Don't Become The Victim

Don't Become The Victim

by Marcus Wayne Ratledge

Paladin Press
Boulder, Colorado

Don't Become the Victim

Published by Paladin Press, a division of
Paladin Enterprises, Inc., P.O. Box 1307, Boulder, CO 80306

ISBN 0-87364-211-2
Printed in the United States of America

First Edition

To my mother, Nora Mae Ratledge, whose love never wavered.

To my sister, Beverly Garrett, whose faith and confidence inspired this work.

To Andra Kaye Catron, who gave me five years of happiness and taught me how to love.

To my friend, Mrs. Anne Carlo, without whose gift this book could not have been completed.

Especially dedicated to Allen and Bobby.

Contents

Preface

Each year, over $20 billion are lost to crime in the United States—a sum far greater than the combined net profits of America's twenty-five largest corporations. Even this astronomical amount does not account for the inconveniences caused to victims of property crimes such as auto theft and burglary, nor for the trauma suffered by murder, rape, and assault victims. Furthermore, the statistics do not indicate the moral decay of our country due to so-called victimless crimes such as prostitution, gambling, and narcotics addiction.

This book seeks to explore every common crime, its causes, and most importantly, its prevention. This is not merely a "take your keys out of your car," or "leave a light on when you leave home" crime prevention book. Rather, it provides a critical analysis of each crime, and a detailed blueprint for its prevention. Many of these prevention techniques are simple and inexpensive, while others can be relatively complex and costly. When confronting crime, it is not always possible to have the best of both worlds: security and convenience. Often, one must be sacrificed for the other. Still, if these directions and suggestions are followed, the reader can greatly reduce the chances of being victimized.

The information that follows is based on my twenty years of personal experience as a professional thief, and also includes knowledge drawn from the thousands of diverse criminals I have encountered both out of and in prison, where I am today. Yet since coming to prison, I have realized the senselessness of my misdeeds and am planning a significantly different course for my life upon release.

This volume, then, represents the beginning of my new career, and marks the end of the life I once lived. And it is my greatest desire that those who read this book use this information so that they, too, *don't become the victim.*

Introduction

All of us, at one time or another, heard the myth that crime doesn't pay. A myth? you ask. Yes, a myth. For every time a crime is committed, someone pays. Not only those who have automobiles stolen, homes burglarized, businesses robbed, or themselves or their loved ones ravished at the hands of a rapist. But each one of us, every time anyone makes a purchase large or small, repays part of the over $20 billion lost annually to crimes against property in the United States alone.

But don't the criminals themselves also pay for their misdeeds? To this grave question our law enforcement officials only hang their heads and utter a reluctant no. It is a fact that 79 percent of all those who violate our laws escape apprehension. *Impossible!* you say. Even though this is the computer age, and our police agencies are armed with the finest equipment, *must we all still live in fear? But what can be done?* Nothing.

Absolutely nothing, that is, unless you as an individual take proper action to protect your personal property and your life. For if you continue along life's path as you have previously, you are merely waiting out the dwindling odds that control whether you will become the victim of crime. If you do indeed become such a victim and do *not* know what to do, you may become an ultimate victim—of homicide.

There is one rule here which generally applies to the

public at large: it leaves itself vulnerable to crime. And since opportunity often prompts courage, resulting in a crime committed by someone with a clean record, unknowingly *we* are actually encouraging the commission of crimes.

Most of those who steal are not hardened criminals and are not willing to take more than minimum risk. They usually will steal only what is readily available. In fact, fewer than 5 percent of those who steal are true professionals. This small percentage take stealing seriously and work at the "profession" as diligently as doctors or attorneys. Stealing to a pro is essentially a matter of economics. Lack of formal education or vocation, or outright laziness prevents him from earning enough money honestly to live as he desires. Generally, the professional criminal will equip himself equally, and in many instances superiorly, to the local police force that protects his territory of operations. And when he does execute a crime, it is usually with devastating effectiveness.

In *Don't Become the Victim,* I present an inside view of this criminal world to which you are a stranger. Indeed it is a sad day when citizens believe that every thought and action must be defensive, when personal security depends on what is affordable, when homes must become veritable fortresses. Yet such heavy-handed protective measures are not always the answer, or even desirable. Self-confidence and common-sense precautions can go a long way towards crime prevention; expensive electronic systems often do no more than burn a hole in the owner's pocket.

1. Auto Theft

Ever since Mr. Daimler of Germany produced the first automobile in 1887, auto theft has grown steadily with each year's increased production. Making the situation even more depressing is the fact that until 1968 very little preventive action was taken on the production level. It was in 1968 that the hue and cry from the public and consumer organizations drew the attention of Congress, which subsequently passed legislation forcing the automobile makers to meet minimum antitheft requirements.

But with over a million automobiles stolen annually, the burden of prevention must also be shared by the individual owner.

Amateurs and Joyriders

There are many reasons why automobiles are stolen, joyriding being the most capricious of all. Joyriders are usually thrill-seeking young people who find a car complete with the keys, steal it, and then drive it around town hot-rodding until their time, money, or gas runs out. At which time they will abandon the stolen car and walk or ride the bus back home, ending the night's fun.

If you are a fortunate victim in this case, your car will be found by the police in a day or two, somewhat abused but in one piece. But most of the time you will not be so lucky. In the hands of a joyrider the chances of your auto becoming involved in an accident are increased fivefold!

Transients are also known for stealing cars. Perhaps a hitchhiker is tired of walking in the wind, the rain, and the cold. Servicemen on leave or AWOL are also infamous for unauthorized auto-borrowing. They will find an easy-to-steal car, usually with the keys in it, and drive it to where they are going. These people are apt to take better care of a car than a joyrider, mainly for fear of being stopped by police or breaking down prior to reaching their destination.

When one of the transient-stolen autos is discovered a week or two later, 200 to 3,000 miles from where it was stolen, the owner is faced with the problem and expense of recovery, providing his insurance does not cover the cost.

Preventing these types of auto theft is very simple. Technically these people are not real thieves—culprits, yes; thieves, no. They are merely taking advantage of a situation. Your actions may determine the destiny of one who might not otherwise take that first step toward thievery.

There are essentially a half-dozen rules which, if observed, will greatly reduce the possibility of these thefts.

Never leave a car running while you are going into a store or house, even if only for a minute. Not even if you have left a dog, or especially a child, in the car. A thief in a hurry may not notice the child until he is several miles away. When he does discover the child, he may just abandon the auto and its infant passenger in hopes it will be discovered. But if the car is not found immediately, the child may die from exposure.

Always remove the keys and lock the doors when getting out of a car. If your car is stolen because the keys were left in it, many insurance companies will not pay your claim if the auto is not recovered. Even if the company does pay, it will most likely cancel your policy, making it extremely difficult to obtain another policy, and then only at a higher rate. Locking the doors will stall a thief and help protect the property within as well. The longer the thief has to work at stealing a car, the greater his possibility of being caught. More often than not he will pass over your locked auto for one unlocked. And be assured there will be plenty to choose from.

Take care of your spare. If you must carry a second set of keys, do not leave them under the floor mat or the seat, or in the ashtray, glove compartment, or console. Forty-one percent of the cars stolen each year are driven away with spare keys, and these areas are the first places a thief will look. A billfold or handbag is a more suitable place for such spares.

When the little magnetic boxes for hiding keys outside of a car were introduced several years ago, they were bought by the millions. Purchasers were sure they had the perfect hiding places for their boxes. Yet these boxes have aided car thieves more than any single item ever put on the market. Placing one under a door, fender well or hood of an automobile is an invitation to a thief.

When parking at night, leave your vehicle as close to a light as possible. If it is not dark when you park, but will be before you return, look for lighting fixtures and park accordingly.

When parking in the daytime, do not park in an isolated area where the general public cannot see it. An auto not easily visible is twice as likely to be stolen or vandalized.

Be extra careful when parking near a bowling alley, golf course, sports event, theater, or beauty parlor where the thief can estimate how long you will be gone.

A car should never be abandoned on the expressway. Instead, signal for assistance with a white handkerchief tied on the driver's door or radio antenna. With the widespread use of citizen band radios, help should arrive shortly. An abandoned auto may be found by a mechanically-inclined thief able to repair problems you cannot. A special note to the female reader: there is also the possibility of a rapist catching you after leaving your car on a dark highway. In the auto you can at least lock the doors and roll up the windows.

And last, most auto thefts occur in residential districts, over 50 percent of them at night. Therefore, *cars should always be locked, even when parked in driveways or garages.*

These simple steps will reduce the threat of theft by 85 percent.

Automobile theft for personal use is not uncommon. By *personal use* I mean the thief drives the auto as if it were his own, until either he is apprehended or the car breaks down through abuse or age. The car is then discarded. These thefts usually occur after a person has been unsuccessful in purchasing transportation due to bad credit or lack of funds. In many cases, after his own car has broken down through age or accident, he will replace his disabled machine with a stolen one preferably of the same model and color. However, these cases usually are quickly solved, since the thief has neither the knowledge nor the equipment to successfully transform a stolen auto into legitimate, titled transportation.

Criminal Complications

The use of stolen trucks and cars in the commission of criminal acts, such as robbery and burglary, is an old practice. The use of two or more vehicles in a single crime is not unusual. Most of these are recovered soon after the crime is committed. If there has been no confrontation with the police, such as a shoot-out or chase, the auto will probably be in the same condition as when stolen. This does not necessarily mean the auto will be returned immediately to the owner. First the car must be taken to the crime laboratory to be checked for fingerprints and other evidence. If the auto was involved in a crime during which a homicide occurred, the car could be impounded as evidence and kept for months or even years.

During this time the owner is without an automobile. Most insurance companies will not furnish the unfortunate owner with another car, since the auto is no longer stolen. The police certainly cannot furnish a replacement auto since they are not at fault. To add insult to injury, the owner may be asked to establish an alibi, especially if the actual criminal is not captured immediately. Once the criminal is caught, the owner may be asked, or required, to appear in court as a witness. This whole procedure is a terrible waste of time and money, which can easily be avoided.

Parking for a Price

When leaving an auto at a parking lot or garage, never assume it will just be parked and left undisturbed until you return. Many parking attendants are also employees of auto theft rings, suppliers of stolen cars and keys to amateur thieves (professionals steal their own) who use them to commit various crimes, and dealers of stolen guns and credit cards taken from the cars they park.

To the auto theft rings, the attendants will supply names, addresses, and sometimes duplicate keys of cars which are in great demand or difficult to find. The actual theft takes place at the owner's residence, therefore casting no suspicion upon the parking lot. For his assistance, the attendant receives from five to twenty dollars.

The attendant who is not so discreet will supply, for a percentage of the take, cars to amateur thieves to commit robberies and burglaries while the owners are away. This setup is very risky, and therefore rare, since much can go wrong. Should the borrower be apprehended or the owner return prematurely, of course the attendant will claim the auto somehow was mysteriously stolen.

Unscrupulous attendants also supply work schedules and house keys of a car's owner to burglars so homes can be burglarized easily while the owner is definitely known to be gone.

Guns and credit cards are also a booming business for the crooked parking attendant. When he finds an auto with a gun in it, he will acquire the address of the owner and sell the information to another thief. Or he steals it himself, and sells it on the lucrative illegal gun market.

The going price for stolen credit cards is twenty-five dollars each. The ambitious attendant with a flair for searching and stealing from cars can easily make from $300 to $1,000 a week. Almost everyone who carries credit cards has at least one in the glove compartment or console, both of which people tend to leave unlocked. Many other card-owners carelessly leave them in the ashtray or on the dash.

If you will read the fine print on the back of your credit card or on its application, you will find you are not responsible for any purchase made "after" the card is "reported" stolen. So if you do not notice the theft at once and the user is not captured, the result could be a financial catastrophe for you.

Therefore, when parking at a lot or garage, insist on parking your own car and removing the keys yourself, if possible. If that is not possible, wait until the car is parked and have the keys brought to you.

An address tag should never be placed on a key ring. If the keys are lost, you are telling the finder "here are my house and car keys and my address," not to mention letting every parking attendant in town know where you live.

Leaving credit cards and guns in a car is asking for

trouble. Carrying credit cards on your person may not be as convenient as reaching in the glove compartment, console or dash, but it may save you many tears.

A car is the worst place in the world to leave a gun, death row excepted. Always remove guns from the interior and place them in the trunk if you must leave them in the car unattended. Over half the handguns in the hands of criminals today were stolen from automobiles.

Professional Auto Theft Rings

Of all the different types of car thieves, organized automobile theft rings are by far the most feared by owners, police, and insurance companies alike. Once a car falls into these hands the chance of recovering it in original condition is almost zero. Never doubt that these auto theft rings are extremely professional multimillion-dollar businesses.

In 1963 the government formed the National Auto Theft Bureau (NATB). This nationally coordinated effort to enact title and salvage laws in previously non-title states uncovered organized theft rings and put a dent in their business. It eliminated many of the smaller rings and a few of the larger ones. The government will not, however, effectively control these rings as long as people are willing to make such a major purchase *without bothering to inquire into its origin.* And for every car stolen and resold by an auto theft ring, there are often two victims: the person from whom the car was originally stolen, and the person who then bought it.

One type of theft ring specializes in stealing cars for parts. The sheet metal is sold to auto body-fender shops to be installed on wrecked autos. The mechanical parts are distributed through motor and transmission rebuilders, garages, parts houses, and service stations. The upholstery is sold to shops handling this merchandise.

Believe it or not, most of these rings operate on a pre-order basis. Here a body shop will place an order with a theft ring for a certain make, model, and year of car needed to repair a customer's wrecked vehicle. The ring then will check with other businesses needing mechanical auto parts, and try to match their needs to the unwanted parts that will also be stripped from the car ordered. In effect, the ring will attempt to fill two orders with one stolen car. Since only the parts which are (or can be made) unidentifiable are used and the remains destroyed, these organizations are all but impenetrable. Autos which disappear through their efforts are rarely recovered, in any form.

The auto theft rings which transform stolen automobiles into seemingly legitimate transportation, and then sell them to the general public, are the best organized of all. They are capable of stealing an auto, changing all necessary serial numbers, financing, and selling it to an unsuspecting buyer before it is ever reported stolen. These rings deal primarily, but not exclusively, in new and one-year-old luxury and high-performance cars. The process of transforming and selling such cars goes somewhat as follows.

The process begins in the states with no laws governing the sale of totally wrecked automobiles. A member of the theft ring will purchase the newest totally wrecked cars available, regardless of their condition, from insurance salvage pools or junk yards. As soon as the wreck is purchased, the ring member will contact a professional car thief and give him the make and model of the car needed to take advantage of the newly acquired title. The thief will then steal and deliver the desired car to an illicit rebuilder. By this time the rebuilder has already received the wrecked car's title, registration papers, license plate, Vehicle Identification Number (VIN) plate from its dash, and a list of all the hidden numbers from the salvage man. The rebuilder then goes to work exchanging the two VIN plates and altering the hidden numbers of the stolen car to match those of the auto purchased from the salvage dealer. When this work is completed, the stolen car is by all appearances no longer a stolen auto, but the wrecked one which was purchased as salvage, in many cases within the same day.

The car is then passed on to a salesman who will find a buyer. Which is where you, the customer, come into the picture. There are three ways for the salesman to sell a stolen car: at an auto auction, to an automobile dealership, or through the classified ad section of the newspaper. Selling to a used car dealer is risky, since most are suspicious of extremely good deals and often check a car's background before purchasing it. Occasionally, a dealer will unknowingly purchase a stolen auto. If the consumer purchases an auto from a dealer which later proves to be stolen, the dealer can be held liable.

Public auctions are a favorite place for disposing of stolen autos. Since these auctions are usually held at night when state offices are closed, the purchaser cannot check into the background of the seller or the car. If the car later turns out to be stolen, the auction cannot be held responsible since it is just a mediator. If the purchaser cannot locate the seller, he has no recourse. He must relinquish the car to the original owner, or to the insurance company if it has already paid the owner, and take the loss.

The most direct way to sell stolen cars is through the classified ads in local newspapers. Here, the seller rents an apartment or house under an alias that matches the name on the title of the stolen car. Quickly the seller arranges to have a telephone installed in the new residence. He then places two "for sale" advertisements in the local newspaper listing two cars, $500 to $1,000 below their actual market values.

When callers answer the advertisements the seller explains that he and his wife have two cars and must sell one. But as soon as he makes a sale, he brings in another stolen car which has been changed over to appear legitimate, and places another ad for it in the newspaper. Part of his plan is to always have two cars for sale at once. After making ten to fifteen sales, he will vanish without a trace, only to reappear in a new apartment under a new identity.

Many unsuspecting persons purchase stolen automobiles in exactly this manner, only to learn at a later date that the car was stolen. But what happens when a person learns he has invested his hard-earned money in a hot car? He will probably begin by telling the police. They will investigate every aspect of the transaction to learn if the buyer knew the car was stolen. In any case, the purchaser must immediately return the car to the rightful owner or insurance company. If the buyer can locate the seller, he can demand his money be returned or hire an attorney and sue. But if the seller cannot be found, which is usually the case, all is lost.

To make the situation even more delicate, if law enforcement officials are not completely satisfied you did not know the car was stolen, you may face a grand jury indictment. If indicted, you will face a jury trial for possession of stolen merchandise. The state of Michigan now has a law in effect which makes it a felony for anyone to pay less than 50 percent of the market value for any merchandise—the assumption being that anyone paying such a low price surely must suspect the merchandise to be stolen.

If the purchaser has borrowed money to pay for the car, he must still repay the loan as if he still had possession of the car. Unfair? Yes and no. From the bank's standpoint, it is not unfair. It is not the bank's fault the customer bought a stolen car. To the victim, yes, it is unfair. However, had the buyer taken the time to make a few simple inquiries and telephone calls, this entire, unfortunate episode could have been avoided.

So when purchasing a used auto, regardless of the source, be sure to check into the background of both the seller and the car. If purchasing from an individual, find out how long the seller has lived at his present address. (Ask the landlord, not the seller.) How long has the seller owned the car? This information can be obtained from the title and registration papers. If he is a new owner, *beware.* Stolen autos are almost without exception second- or third-owner cars.

The best check to make on a car is to call the previous owner, *especially* if he lives in another state, and ask about the condition of the car when it was sold. If you are told the car was wrecked when it was sold, you are probably looking at a stolen auto. Even if it hasn't been stolen, you certainly don't want to buy a car which has been wrecked. So just thank yourself you had the good sense to check before buying, and go look for another car. If the car is given a clean bill of health, don't feel foolish. After all, it's your money!

Maximum Protection

The automobile industry has yet to produce a car which a professional thief cannot steal. For the last decade the auto makers have been installing ignition key warning buzzers, locking steering columns and transmissions, and harder-to-reach door handles and locking buttons. Each year innovations are added, some with a measure of success. Ford Motor Company was the first to install steering column locks which would break away the outer portion, leaving the locking mechanism intact, if forcible removal is attempted. This makes it more difficult for the thief to unlock the steering column and turn on the ignition.

Many auto makers also now offer factory installed burglar alarms. Unlike add-on devices sold by independent companies, these alarms do not have the telltale activating switch on the fender or door. Rather, they are turned on and off by the regular front door locks.

There are also many other antitheft devices built into the various model lines which are not visible, and to reveal them would be giving the amateurs an edge they would not otherwise have without dismantling the individual models.

However, professional car thieves are well aware of the location of each new antitheft device as well as the quickest way to beat them. Each year as soon as, and sometimes before, the new models are displayed, they will have all necessary information on the new antitheft systems. They also explore each new antitheft device which appears on the shelves of the local auto supply store.

What then, you must be asking yourself, can you do to protect your car from the professional car thief that Detroit and the manufacturers of the antitheft devices cannot? If you will use a little discretion, a touch of logic, add a few dollars and keep a secret, you can do a great deal.

But first let's look at the devices which are presently on the market, and examine why they are inadequate. Most of these devices are labled "Auto Burglar Alarm." That is just what they are: burglar alarms. Not antitheft devices. They are wonderful for scaring away nervous thieves who wish to steal articles from inside the car, or parts such as the battery from under the hood or the spare tire from the trunk. But the alarms will do very little to prevent a determined thief from stealing the car. Perhaps if I explain how these systems work, you can understand why they *don't* work.

Most systems consist of from four to six button-type switches attached under the hood, trunk, and in the jamb of each door. A key lock on/off switch is placed outside of the car and must be turned on each time the car is left unattended for the alarm to work. When the alarm is on and the hood or trunk raised or a door opened, the car's horn or an optional siren will sound off. But, on many of these systems, as soon as the opening is closed, the alarm will stop sounding. In this case, you would either have to be close enough to hear the alarm, or be so fortunate as to have a thief stupid enough to leave the door ajar and attract someone's attention who knows who owns the car.

Other systems will continue to sound the alarming device, even though the opening has been closed, until it is reset with a key. Here the thief merely cuts the wires at the on/off switch, or raises the hood and quickly cuts the wires leading to the alarm device.

These alarms sell for as little as $15 to as much as $130. I would certainly not recommend any of them to anyone seeking an antitheft device for an automobile.

I know of only one good, inexpensive, and simple antitheft system which is practically foolproof. This is the installment of a switch which prevents the engine from being started unless it, as well as the regular ignition switch, is turned on. The switch is connected between the ignition switch and the engine with regular electrical wire. The switch itself is positioned in a convenient, yet unobservable, place such as just under the edge of the dash, seat, or door armrest. Caution should be exercised to assure no telltale wires are exposed which may allow the thief to trace them to the location of the switch. *Never* put a switch where it can be easily seen or located, such as on or in the console, or on the steering column or dash.

Anyone who does not know the location of the switch cannot start the engine even though he has the proper keys to the ignition switch. This system can be installed by a good, trustworthy mechanic for about five or ten dollars and should not take longer than thirty minutes. It is a small price to pay for the peace of mind which comes with knowing your automobile will always be exactly where you left it whenever you return.

Certainly the professional thief knows of these switches, but he will not take the time to look for the switch since the starting problem could be mechanical failure as well as contrived. But if you are foolish enough to put this additional switch in an obvious location, you will only defeat its purpose.

Last, but most important, if you install a cutoff switch, by all means turn it *off* whenever you leave your car.

The Automotive Dealership

Automotive dealerships are the most vulnerable of all businesses to amateur as well as professional car thieves. They are targets mainly because an auto stolen at night or on weekends may not be missed or reported for hours or days. But what amazes this security conscious observer is the dealerships continue to lose cars year after year, never realizing their mistakes and therefore taking no preventive measures. Many honest, hard-working dealers have found themselves in serious financial trouble and even bankruptcy due to repeated thefts.

After the first or second theft the insurance agency usually cancels their policy. They cannot find another insurer willing to take the risk of carrying them. Had they taken a few inexpensive preventive measures, not only would they have avoided losses, but their insurance would have remained active, often at a lower premium. Many insurance companies have realized this problem and now require that minimum standards be met.

As a matter of customer convenience, a dealer usually places all necessary keys in every auto at the beginning of each workday. Prospective customers may browse at will through the cars without a salesman present to fetch keys from the office as each car is inspected. This procedure is a common mistake. It leaves the thief with the simple task of borrowing the keys, making a duplicate, and returning the originals before they are missed. When the dealership is closed he will return and drive away in the selected car.

If a dealer places two sets of keys in the cars, he is making the theft even easier. The thief will merely remove one set and replace them with a phony set. Many professional thieves carry at least one set for every make of auto, especially those in great demand.

The best way to retain good customer service as well as prevent key theft and duplication is to place a single ignition key, which on most cars also opens the doors, on a large key ring which can be seen at a distance. By placing the key in the exterior door lock, employees can spot a missing key by glancing over the lot. At the end of the day when the keys are removed, each one should be checked. If a key will not open the corresponding lock, or if a key is missing, a report should be made to the local authorities at once.

The theft of keys, however, is only half the problem which dealers face. A professional does not need a key, though it does make his work easier. But once a car is started it must be driven off the lot. Again the dealer makes this too accessible. Most lots are open—no chains, fences or barriers to prevent theft. Many dealers do not even seal exits when closed. This allows the thief to drive simply off the curb or out the exit.

Preventive measures are not always cheap, depending on the size of the dealership. But there is one security layout providing maximum protection, without distracting greatly from the beauty of the property, all for minimum of cost.

Lengths of pipe, 3½ feet long with three-inch outside diameters, concreted two feet into the ground at four-feet intervals around the entire circumference, will prevent any drive-out. Pipe is cheaper and more suitable than a wall or fence of equal height. A fence can be cut easily and a wall quickly destroyed by driving against it or knocking it down with a sledge hammer.

To seal exits, a heavy chain can be arc welded to the pipe on one side and secured by the strongest padlock available on the other. The chain should be hung at a height of approximately two feet, too low to drive under and too high to drive over. I cannot overemphasize the importance of a strong lock and chain. A good pair of bolt cutters will shear through most of the chains and locks on today's market. An anchor chain of the type used on large boats is one exception. These heavy-duty chains can be purchased sometimes at reasonable prices from navy surplus stores or new from marine dealers. The Master Seven, or its equivalent in the Yale line, upward, is a good place to start shopping for padlocks.

This method of securing exits is much better than blocking them with other vehicles, since those too can be easily moved or stolen. There have been cases where the thief moved four or five cars before stealing the one he wanted. Blocked exits do not create a major problem for the determined thief.

Daytime theft from dealerships is not common, but it does occur. The thief will usually select a busy moment and ask permission to try a certain car. Dealers who will not permit solo tryouts if a customer walks in, sometimes will grant permission to others who drive in. This is also a serious mistake, because the thief can just keep going. In this case, the thief will steal another car and drive it into the lot under the pretense of trading for a newer model. If he is allowed to try the car alone, he will leave the stolen car behind and keep the new car the dealer so foolishly allowed him to drive.

Taking Recreational Vehicles Seriously

The public buys camper trailers and boats by the thousands. Anything the public will buy, a thief will steal. Many states have not yet written title laws for these vehicles. Even worse, some states do not even require serial numbers to be recorded on registration papers or bills of sale presented to obtain registrations and license plates. In these states the vehicles are almost untraceable, making thefts very difficult to solve.

These thefts usually occur when campers or boats are parked at owners' residences or at dealerships. Strangely enough, factories which produce these vehicles do not install any type of antitheft devices. Property protection is the owner's responsibility.

There are only a few ways to protect boats and campers. The simplest is to drill a quarter-inch hole in the hitch of the trailer, where the ball locks within. Lock a heavy-duty padlock into the hole, preventing anyone from hooking up a hitch and pulling it away. But remember the bolt cutters and the importance of a strong padlock.

The surest way to prevent theft is also the cheapest. It takes little time and energy. All you have to do is jack up your trailer, and remove the wheel or wheels from one side. Remove the jack, leaving the trailer on wooden blocks. If the trailer will not be moved for a long period of time, all wheels can be removed.

Letting the air out of the tires has the same effect in theory, but not so in fact. First, the weight of the trailer may pinch and puncture the tubes. Second, thieves who make their living stealing recreational vehicles are well aware of this trick and carry a portable air tank to inflate the tires. However, only one thief in a million will go to the trouble of measuring the hub, and the expense of purchasing new wheels, tires, and tubes. He will pass you by in favor of the many who laughed at the prospect of someone stealing something as large and bulky as a camper trailer or boat and left the wheels intact.

2. Burglary

Burglary is the most frequent crime in the United States today. Burglaries average one every twelve seconds, twenty-four hours each day, 365 days a year. With an annual increase of 9 percent, and only one out of ten being solved, there can be only one explanation for such statistics: burglary is a crime made so easy even the novice thief cannot resist it. To protect your home and business against burglars, you must first understand the burglar himself and why and how he selects his victims.

The burglar is looking for cash and merchandise which can be stolen with a minimum of risk, a maximum number of escape routes, and absolutely no confrontation. He should not be taken lightly. If armed he should be considered dangerous. The very worst thing a victim can do is catch him in the act. After all, that is why he is a burglar instead of a robber: he does not want a witness who can identify him.

The decision whether or not the burglar will follow through with the act after selecting a particular site, unless he is semiprofessional or professional, will depend on one factor—*risk,* not the value of the property to be stolen. Although the lure of money or valuable merchandise may have drawn him to the scene, he will not make an attempt to take it if the risk involved is equal to or greater than his ability.

If you, the prospective victim, increase the risk above the ability of novice and amateur thieves, you can rest assured your property is reasonably safe. I will concede that your security depends to a degree on what you can afford and are willing to pay. But your greatest degree of security will be obtained by the judgment you exercise when executing preventive action, most of which costs absolutely nothing.

In Broad Daylight

There are two kinds of burglars—those who strike during the daylight hours, and those who prefer darkness. Each kind is different and must be dealt with accordingly.

The daylight thief is usually the novice or amateur. He is probably two months behind on his rent, three months overdue with his car payment, has taken a few drinks or dropped a couple pills, and may be struggling to support a drug habit. He may cruise the streets for an hour searching for a suitable victim and building up his nerve. As he drives he surveys houses for a sign that indicates the owner is not home. After a while he finds a quiet street and slows down. He sees a rolled-up newspaper in the front yard, closed drapes, the open and empty garage. He looks for dogs, dog houses, and children's toys and sees none.

Nervously he pulls into the driveway, stops just inside the garage, and walks to the back door. He finds a note attached to the screen saying, "Gone shopping, be back around noon, Mom." He rings the bell several times and gets no reply. He tries the door knob. Finding it locked, he goes back to his car and returns with a crowbar. Quickly he jimmies the door and goes inside.

The neighbor who lives across the street was looking out her window and saw the young man get out of a strange car and go around to the back of the house. She shrugs her shoulders. Why should she care what happens to Mrs. Jones' house? Mrs. Jones wouldn't even offer to pay for the tulips she ran over yesterday backing out of her driveway. She goes back to watching Merv Griffin on TV.

Meanwhile, the burglar is searching the house for anything which can be quickly sold. He takes a color television from the living room, a black-and-white portable from the den, a component stereo and portable radio from the teen-ager's room, and stacks it all by the door. He decides to take another look to make sure he hasn't missed anything valuable. In the master bedroom he finds two shotguns and three suits in the closet, a .38 caliber revolver between the mattresses, and six dollars and a Sears credit card in the bottom of a jewelry box. He runs to the back door and carries the merchandise to the car.

When the last piece is stuffed into the back seat, the color television hanging half out of the trunk, he backs out of the driveway. He reaches the street and spins his tires in haste. The noise brings the neighbor across the street to her window. He was in the house for less than two minutes.

The neighbor sees the strange car racing up the street with the television in the trunk and wonders if the man was a television repair man or a thief. She shrugs again. Who cares? If he is a thief, it will serve Mrs. Jones right for running over her tulips.

The situation just described is not at all fictional. Many thieves have made their debut into crime in exactly this manner. About half will remain in this class. They are working at their maximum ability. They continue on this level until they quit, are apprehended, or get killed. These thieves always select only the homes and apartments where the owners advertise that they are not at home.

Let us go back over what our thief looks for and why.

A newspaper on the front porch or lawn at nine o'clock in the morning says the owner left for work before the paper arrived or in such a hurry he did not have time to read it. Anyone at home surely would have brought the paper inside.

Draperies that are closed at mid-morning or later also indicate the house is deserted. The only draperies which should remain drawn during the daylight hours are the ones over the door windows. When a thief cannot see through a door, there is a certain mystery created. It leaves a question in his mind as to whether or not someone is actually home.

A garage door left open when no one is present is like a green light to a thief. Not only will he assume that, since no vehicle is present, the occupants are away, but they may have been in such a hurry when they departed they forgot to lock doors or turn on their burglar alarm, if they have one. A closed garage door, on the other hand, engenders doubt in the thief's mind. If a house has a carport instead of a garage, there is always a doubt, simply because the house always looks the same when no one is at home. Unless there are other revealing signs, the house always looks occupied.

The presence of toys, tricycles, and bicycles with training wheels means small children. Because small children must always have someone to watch them, it means only trouble to the thief, not only at the house where the toys are located, but all surrounding houses as well. People tend to live in neighborhoods with those of equal maternal as well as economic and social status. In short, a thief knows where there are a few children, there are usually many.

Dogs, especially large ones (they make more noise), are the best overall house protection one can have. Even many professional burglars will turn away from a house which has a dog guarding it. A Doberman pinscher, German shepherd, Siberian husky, chow, and bulldog can cover more area, detect, and defend better and cheaper than anything man has ever invented.

There are, however, a few adaptations dog owners can make to increase protection potential. A dog can guard better inside a house than outside, unless you have a fence surrounding the entire house within which the dog can move freely. But since no one wants to lock a dog inside the house all day, that presents a problem. The easiest and best solution is to install a pet door in the door leading to the fenced area. This will give the dog the freedom of the yard and the owner the protection of the house.

Some people who do not want dogs, for one reason or another, have tried to simulate (with limited success) this kind of protection by playing repetitious recordings of dogs snarling and barking when they are away. Of course the volume must be adjusted so as not to disturb the neighbors and a new recording purchased as the old one wears out. But some feel it is easier than caring for and feeding a dog.

Most burglars can read. Therefore, leaving a note on an outside door when you are going away is only telling the burglar how long he has to remove the contents of your house. If the note can be seen from the street, it is a sure invitation. The refrigerator door is a much better place for such notes since the kitchen is usually the first place one goes when entering a home.

Neighbors are also wonderful watchdogs, if you remain on good terms with them. Almost everyone knows the people and cars of the neighborhood. If each cooperates with the other, collectively they can have a very effective security arrangement. While a neighbor should never try to apprehend a suspect, he can call the police and give them a description of the suspect, his car, and his license number. A citizen's arrest looks good in the newspaper and on television, but is the worst possible action one can attempt. It could result in being listed in the obituary column instead of becoming a hero. *This job belongs to the police.* Many innocent people have lost their lives for only surprising burglars, much less trying to arrest one. To emphasize this is the fact that 110 policemen have been killed in the last ten years pursuing or trying to arrest burglary suspects.

If you come home and find a burglar inside, and he does not see you first, get away from the house as quickly and quietly as possible. Go to the nearest telephone and call the police. If you notice signs of forced entry or evidence of burglary, but do not see the burglar, do not go inside—call the police.

When coming face to face with a burglar, you must remember you are now a robbery victim with the possibility of becoming a homicide victim. Your actions may very well determine if you will be alive after the thief has departed. Remaining calm is the key to survival in this kind of situation. Never scream or try to get away unless you are sure you can escape. Otherwise, the attempt will only get you hurt. Do exactly as you are told—no more, no less. If he wants you to help load the silver your mother gave you on your wedding day into his car, do it. If he wants you to sing, then sing. But don't make him angry. Burglars, as a rule, do not want to hurt people, but this does not mean they are not capable of it.

If these suggestions are followed, the chances of daytime burglary will be cut 75 percent, almost entirely eliminating the novice and amateur thieves.

Under Cover of Night

Prevention of nighttime burglary follows much the same lines as daytime prevention, with a few variations. Draperies should be closed and windows covered completely to cut out all view from outside. Then, if no light is on inside, the burglar is left to wonder if the occupants are away or have already retired for the night. If a light is on, provided it is not a small one just inside the entrance, it could mean the family is having a quiet evening at home.

The best invitation you can give a burglar is to leave a light burning just inside the entrance, and no other. To a burglar this means you left a light on when you went away so you could see your way inside when you return without stumbling over something. A porch light on with no other interior light burning means the same. On the other hand, if several inside lights are on in separate locations, as well as the exterior lights, the intruder may think the house is occupied and the occupants expecting company.

The best lights left on when leaving home are the porch light, bathroom light, overhead bedroom light in a different part of the house, and a television playing in the living room or den.

The bathroom light is very important, mainly because it is the one light everyone turns off when leaving home. Bathroom windows can easily be found from outside of the house, since they are usually smaller, higher, or set alone. They are the first places a burglar will look when in doubt.

The bedroom light in a different part of the house will give the impression of two or more people being inside the home.

A television is most important, especially if it can be seen by looking in an outside door. When scenes in the program change, the lighting in the room also changes. From the outside, this gives the effect of someone moving about in front of a light. If the television can be seen from an outside door, it will cast a strong doubt in the mind of the thief as to whether or not there are people watching it even if he cannot see anyone.

If you arrive home habitually after nightfall, consider photoelectric light switches which automatically turn lights on at sunset and off at sunrise. They can be purchased at any electronics supply store for about four dollars each and placed in any desired location.

Protective lighting as described will cost about five cents for each night used in the average-sized home, a security measure well within any family budget.

The Professional Burglar

Competing against experienced amateurs and professional burglars is more complex and costly. While the amateur selects victims at random, the professional discriminates. He is drawn to the victims by advance knowledge of prospective valuables. This will include not only currency, but coin and stamp collections, jewelry, rare Persian rugs, antiques, tapestries, and works of art. He steals for profit, not merely for survival. He is usually the most intelligent, cunning, and clever kind of thief. He understands people—their habits, weaknesses, and faults.

Television and movies have produced an image of the burglar which is far from true. He is seen as a man who can pick any lock, open the best bank vault, and wire around the most sophisticated alarm system. I assure you, this is all only in the script. For there is only one thief in 10,000 who is this accomplished. There are many who claim these accomplishments and a few who have some knowledge of their mechanics. But most criminals will never exert the energy, expense, and time required to master such skills. So the chance of encountering a true professional burglar in your lifetime is about as remote as finding a diamond mine in your backyard.

However, there are a few thorns in this bouquet of roses just presented. It is a fact that all locks, safes, and vaults can be opened, although the methods are neither as neat nor noiseless as that of the locksmith.

It is also a fact that 80 percent of all alarms now installed in homes and businesses are of such simplicity any amateur burglar can work around them. But, with slight modifications, these same alarms can be made all but unbeatable.

Why the professional thief selects a particular target depends largely on the information he has gathered. One chief source is the local newspaper. Here he learns of social and family events: where and what time they will be held; who will attend; and what he can expect to find at the abandoned homes of those attending.

Births, marriages, and deaths are published events which are sure to take the entire affected family away from home.

When a baby is born many newspapers will publish the names and addresses of the relatives as well as the parents and the name of the hospital where the birth occurred. This leaves the thief free to check on visiting hours when the family might be away from home.

Weddings are also a popular event for the thief. From the newspapers he learns the times and dates of the reception and rehearsals as well as the wedding itself. If a list of bridesmaids and ushers is given, they also become prospective victims.

Thieves have very little respect for the living and even less for the dead, which is why many knowledgeable people do not list the names of their deceased loved ones in the obituary column. Many thieves watch these listings closely, preferring these occasions over weddings since very few people wear jewelry to funerals. They also know the surviving family members are probably distracted and more apt to be less protective and forget to lock doors and turn on burglar alarms.

Therefore, when listing the above-mentioned announcements, detail no more dates and locations than absolutely necessary.

Most of the information the thief uses, however, comes by way of word-of-mouth. It may come from another thief or convict with whom he was in prison or jail. The crime on which Truman Capote based his best-selling novel, *In Cold Blood,* came about in just this manner. Or the tipoff may come from a jealous "friend" of the prospective victims who has tired of hearing them brag about their worldly goods.

Convicts have a bad habit of fantasizing and bragging about the fantastic crimes they almost pulled off, or about the caper they were planning but were arrested before they could execute it. Sometimes one inmate will tell another of a prospective crime and the listener will adapt the story to include himself and add points to improve the story. Then when he tells the story it will be in the first person. These stories are passed from one inmate to another, from one prison to another, exaggerated more each time.

All old convicts know these stories are probably just exaggerations of facts, or outright lies, told to impress other inmates. Still, inmates leave prisons and jails every day with their heads, and sometimes notebooks, full of these prospective thefts.

Jealousy is more a source of information than any other. It may come from the man with whom you play golf, the woman who works beside you in the factory, or the people who live next door. One person will hear another tell again and again about his stamp or coin collection, the one-carat diamond ring just given or received, or about trying to beat the Internal Revenue Service on income tax by not reporting cash income and keeping it at home.

People tend to tire quickly of hearing others brag, especially if they already feel inferior. So maybe they will mention this bragging to someone else, and he to someone else. With as many thieves and people who know thieves as we have today, somewhere along the line one will hear of it. But by this time the circulating story is of a $200,000 face value coin collection, or a fortune in jewels. And the man who was trying to beat the IRS has money stacked to the ceiling.

When the theft does occur, everyone except the person who started the story is unhappy. The thief gets only a fraction of what he expected. The person who told the thief about the valuables in hopes of getting a cut of the loot learns he gets nothing or very little. The victim has lost his most prized possession. But the person who started the story sits right back and grins and says it serves the big blabbermouth right.

I must stress that *this sequence is not a rarity.* It happens every day. If you will keep your personal business personal, it will reduce drastically the chances of your becoming this kind of victim.

The last source of information has to do with the two previously mentioned. There are people, male or female, who make their living selling information to thieves. The thieves call them the *fingers,* because they point the way. The finger is not necessarily a thief or a former thief, but he or she does have many criminal connections. They must be versatile, and able to adapt to any surroundings from skid row to the very elite. A man may use his ability as a con man to seek out the desired facts. A woman may use her feminine wiles. For all the information the finger supplies which is used, providing it is correct, he or she will receive 10 to 25 percent of the taken gross.

The finger is easily avoided if you do as suggested previously: tell others nothing of your valuables if there is no logical reason for them to know.

If you have taken all precautionary measures I have given and still become a burglary victim, you can safely assume the thief is not an amateur.

Home Burglar Alarms

The best way to assure maximum protection is the proper installation of a burglar alarm system. The system can be simple or sophisticated, cheap or expensive, cover a small portion of the home or its entirety, be installed by a do-it-yourselfer or a professional protection agency. But whatever you decide, if your system is to work with maximum effectiveness and efficiency, it must meet your needs and be installed properly.

When selecting an alarm system, never choose one which does not have a battery back-up system. This will allow the system to remain operative even if the electricity fails or is turned off, which is the most usual method of bypassing an alarm. Since all systems do not offer this option you must insist on it.

There are many fine, long-established protection companies of impeccable honesty and integrity. But there are also many fly-by-night companies formed after the owner has taken a basic correspondence course in burglar alarms. Some not only do poor work, but may sell your security blueprints, complete with cutoff keys, to a burglar.

The best companies take pride in tailoring a system to fit the needs of the customer. They will install the alarm and connect it to the local police station or their own security department whose patrols respond to the alarms as well as the police. American Detective Telegraph (ADT) is such a company. Nationally known, they are considered by most the best company as well as having the hardest systems to beat. Many banks, financial institutions, and jewelry companies contract their services. Installation fees are high, however, and a monthly fee is charged if patrols check the premises periodically and/or the alarm is connected directly to the agency. But the monthly fee is usually small (around fifteen dollars) and the contract specifies the maximum time in which the company *must* respond when the alarm is set off, usually two minutes. (Ten to fifteen minutes is about the best you can expect from your local police.)

The most common type of home burglar alarm is the closed circuit intrusion alarm. This system employs contact switches, usually magnetic, leaf, button, or a combination. The switches are placed on all doors and windows large enough for a thief to enter. While the system is turned on, the alarm will sound if any window or door where a switch is located is opened. The alarm either sounds at the security or police station as described above, or sets off a loud bell or police-type siren which hopefully will scare away the intruder and alert someone who will notify police.

If the bell-siren alarm is used, as 90 percent of the home systems do, the position of the bell or siren is of greatest importance. Placing the device outside the house would seem like the best arrangement since it could be heard better. But this is not the case, and is a mistake made far too often by protection agencies as well as the do-it-yourselfer. If the bell-siren is placed outside the home, the thief has only to cut the wires leading to it or dismantle it.

However, placing the alarm inside the home can triple your protection. Install it near an air vent under the house or in the gables, or inside an unused chimney, where it cannot be reached from the outside without setting off the alarm.

The police-type siren usually can be heard at a greater distance, will attract more attention, and scare away burglars much better than the standard bell. Regardless of which kind is selected, choose one which can be heard for at least 300 yards when installed inside the home.

Proper installation of the individual switches is also important. Neither the switch nor the subsequent wiring should ever be exposed. Place switches within the framework and wiring under molding. There, they will not only look neater and be out of sight of visitors and repairmen, but out of reach of the thief as well.

Exposed switches and wiring can be damaged by accident or small children. Or, the system can be made inactive by visitors or repairmen without leaving obvious signs the owner will notice. Also, the thief can knock out the window glass, unscrew the hardware which holds the switches in place, tape the connectors together so the circuit will not be broken, and raise the window to gain entry.

A one-piece multi-purpose leaf contact switch is best for protecting air vents, casements, awnings, double hung windows, sliding doors, and screens. If installed within the framework the switch cannot be tampered with.

Protection for glass walls and glass sliding doors is simple and inexpensive. *Window foil* is a thin, three-eighths-inch wide strip of electrically conductive foil with adhesive backing for easy installation. A 200-foot roll costs about $3.00. Two *foil connectors* are also needed for each area to connect the foil to the protective circuit, and cost about $1.50 per pair.

The foil should be placed about eight inches in from the border around the entire circumference of the glass and connected to the wiring by the foil connectors at the most convenient point. Then, if the glass is cracked or broken at any point, the foil also will break, setting off the alarm.

The location of the on/off switch is also of vital importance. If the switch is placed outside of the home it should be tamper-proof, which means the alarm will be activated if the covering panel is removed or the switch itself is disconnected in any way other than turning it off with the proper key. But even the tamper-proof switches can be picked.

A delayed-action switch installed inside the house is always better. This type of on/off switch will allow the key holder twenty seconds to leave the protected area after setting the alarm. Another twenty seconds on entrance gives the key holder time to turn off the alarm system before activation, removing one more method the thief might use to bypass the alarm.

If the home system is installed by an alarm company the cost will be in excess of $250, depending on the size of the house, number of windows, doors, and areas to be protected, and what the salesman can talk you into buying.

For the do-it-yourselfer, Eico, Emerson-Rittenhouse, On-Guard, and many other companies produce systems which can be installed in a weekend by almost anyone who can use a hammer, screwdriver, and pliers. Prices range from $50 to $200, depending on the quality of merchandise and the size of the residence. These kits usually include the central nerve center for the system, the alarming device, and enough wiring and switches for two doors and eight to ten windows. To this basic system, you can add up to thirty more alarming locations (windows, doors, etc.), at two to five dollars per location.

The burglar alarm system also can double as a fire alarm with added smoke and fire sensors, or as a robbery alarm (see chapter 3). These sensors cost from two to twenty dollars each and will set off the alarm if smoke is detected by the sensors or the temperature rises to 135°.

Locks

The worst door lock for a home is one with the lock in the center of the doorknob that is locked by just closing the door. These locks can be opened with everything from credit cards to pipe wrenches—*more quickly than with a key.*

The best choice is a deadbolt lock. A deadbolt must

be locked or unlocked with a key from either side. It is called a deadbolt because the long bolt which locks into the door frame is not spring-loaded, and is immovable unless the frame is dismantled. That would take tremendous force, a great deal of noise, and a lot of time—all of which the burglar is not willing to risk. The deadbolt is an additional lock and cannot replace the old doorknob lock.

If a deadbolt lock is added, it should be installed at eye level. This will make it five times more difficult for someone to force open the door than if the lock was waist level.

Sliding Glass Doors

Sliding glass doors, which usually have aluminum frames and poor locking devices, are probably the most prevalent means of entrance. The thin, weak frame makes it almost impossible to install a deadbolt lock, thus presenting the problem of how to keep it locked.

The solution is not to keep it from being unlocked, but to keep it from opening. This can easily be accomplished by placing a cut-off piece of broom handle in the bottom runner of the frame. You should be careful to make sure the broom handle, or whatever is used, fits snugly when the door is completely closed.

Burglar Bars

Burglar bars over windows and doors are not as good as burglar alarms, and will not stop the ambitious intruder unless they are the type used in jails. Even superior bars must be installed properly to be effective. The wrought iron, ornamental burglar bars may look strong and may actually be a deterrent in some cases. However, a burglar with a good pair of bolt cutters can cut them away about as fast as you can trim a hedge. The bars are not only inadequate and expensive, but can detract from the clean lines of a home, unlike burglar alarms. Also, many apartment complexes will not allow their installation, which may be half as expensive as the bars themselves.

If you do use burglar bars, always pick the best quality and never use regular screws or bolts to anchor the bars to the house. Security screws and bolts, which require special tools to remove, can be purchased for about a dime apiece. This will not prevent a burglar from cutting away the bars, obviously, but not all burglars carry bolt cutters.

Business Burglar Alarms

For the businessman, a burglar alarm is a necessity, not a luxury. Operating without one is pure foolishness. Many small businesses have been forced into bankruptcy because they made little or no effort to prepare against theft. In most of these cases, the required protection would have cost less than the repair of the building where the thief entered or less than the deductible on their insurance policy.

Since more locations must be secured in a business than in a home, the installation of business burglar alarms is somewhat different, although many of the same guidelines must be followed. The cost, however, need not be greater than that of installing a burglar alarm system in the average-sized home. In many cases it will cost less.

The first step toward protection for a business is outside lighting. All exposed and unexposed sides of the building should be well lighted. The thief is most likely to make his entry on unexposed and usually unlighted sides. A business with no unexposed sides can be driven around by patrols, and is far less receptive to burglars than one without access. The thief is well aware that no policeman will get out of his patrol car and walk around a building without a sidewalk or driveway, unless he is responding to a call.

The businessman must be careful when installing locks as well as installing alarms. A quick thief can force open a door, dash inside, and steal several thousand dollars worth of merchandise before anyone can respond to the alarm. It is best to have at least two, and preferably three, good locks on each door. For convenience all locks can be made to open with the same key.

The best locations for locks are: one foot below the top of the door, within easy reach; and at the very bottom of the door, but with the locking bolt going into the side of the door frame, never the floor. The burglar can use the floor for leverage to pry open the lock.

If the present door has a lock in the center and only one additional lock is desired, place it at the top. It will be more difficult to open there than it would be in the middle or at the bottom.

As I said earlier, aluminum frame doors are weak, can be bent easily and should be avoided if possible. If not, the locking bolt should go into the door frame at least 2½" when locked.

Many businesses have double doors at the rear of the building for the purpose of loading and unloading merchandise. These doors are simple for the thief to open. The installation of locks as described above will help secure them. But best results can be achieved by running a length of heavy chain through the inside door handles and securing the ends with a good padlock.

When installing a business burglar alarm system, exactly the same procedures should be followed as described for home alarms when securing: all outside doors; windows; large glass areas including glass doors, sliding glass doors, and outside showcase windows; location and installment of on/off switch; selection and location of bell or siren; and battery back-up system.

However, this system is not complete. If the building

has a back or side wall which is not subject to surveillance, or a wall which separates the building from another that is not adequately protected by a burglar alarm system, these areas *must* be protected.

If a burglar attempts to enter through a wall it will be within the first four feet of its height. The best and cheapest way to protect these areas is to run strips of window foil horizontally at four one-foot intervals and connect the foil to the wiring circuit in the same manner as described for glass areas. Then, any breakage of the wall will break the foil and set off the alarm. The cost of securing these walls should not be more than five dollars per wall.

Large air vents are also favored points of entry. These vents can be protected by installing a *trip switch.* This switch features a tightly strung wire crisscrossed over the inside of the opening. Adding pressure on the wire, or cutting the wire, will trip the alarm. The squares formed by the crisscrossed wire should not exceed three inches, nor should the trip switch be accessible from the outside.

Protecting large roof areas is difficult, but necessary, since burglars enter through roofs almost as often as through walls. Again, protection can be obtained with window foil. But be sure to cover the entire roof area by running strips of foil the length of the building at one-foot intervals. For a thirty-by-thirty-foot building it should cost only about fifteen dollars.

If the business has an office where a safe, a strongbox, or any money is kept, this area must be protected also. A regular door-type switch is a must for the office door, but security measures should not stop there. The safe itself can and should become part of the system by placement of a pressure switch on the wall with the safe pushed against it. If the safe is of the square-door or double-door variety, and the burglar is intending to rip it open (the usual method of forcibly opening one), first he will move the safe into a position where it can easily be worked on. By doing so he will relieve the pressure on the switch and set off the alarm.

To protect all safes, including round-door types, against the burglar with the cutting torch, place heat sensors on the inside door of the safe. Any attempt to cut open the safe will set off the alarm.

Ultrasonic Alarms

The ultimate in burglar alarms is the *ultrasonic intrusion alarm.* With the exception of the battery back-up and alarming (bell or siren) device, it is a complete, self-contained unit. It needs only to be plugged into any standard receptacle and the alarming device attached to be made operative. These units use invisible, ultrasonic waves lending blanket coverage to any area of 300 to 1,000 square feet, depending on the capacity of the unit. When a protected area is entered, lights, bell/siren, or both give visual as well as audible alarm. Variable timers allow the alarm to remain sounding for eight seconds to three minutes, or as long as the intruder is being detected. The alarm then recycles to the sensing mode to detect further movement. If the thief attempts to reenter the alarm will sound again.

Accessory terminals permit the unit to be expanded, incorporated into a standard system, or used as an independent back-up for any other system.

The delayed-action on/off switch is standard equipment and allows twenty seconds to leave the protected area after setting the alarm, and the same amount of time to turn off the alarm when entering the area.

The placement of the unit will depend upon the shape and size of the area to be protected. If the area is square, the unit should be positioned in the middle of any wall at a height just above the highest obstacle, display cases, clothes racks, etc.

For rectangular areas, place the unit in the middle of one of the longer walls at the same height.

In an **L**-shaped area, it should be placed on the outside corner of the **L** at the same height.

In large areas which require more than one unit, place units where each one will slightly overlap the area protected by the other.

If a safe is the main object of protection, the unit can be placed on top of the safe or on the floor beside it.

Use of the ultrasonic unit automatically eliminates the need for additional protection for walls, ceilings, and air vents. It is not, however, a replacement for good locks and lighting since these are often deterrents.

Although these units were designed for open areas such as shops, stores, and warehouses, they can be used effectively in homes if properly installed. A central point such as a hallway is an excellent location. A foyer which leads to several parts of the house is also a good station.

Since these unmarked units are only about the size of a shoe box and bear no resemblance to burglar alarms, they will go unnoticed and unrecognized by customers or visitors.

Don't let the name *ultrasonic* scare you away before you look at the price tag. Surprisingly, the cost of these unbeatable units is very small in comparison with other security systems. The unit which offers the smallest coverage, approximately 300 square feet, costs about $60. Larger units with coverage up to 2,000 square feet cost approximately $140 each. All prices exclude battery back-up and alarming device.

Backed with a battery pack to guard against electrical blackouts, these units provide the best protection of any system on the market today. They are the toughest system for even the professional burglar to beat and have fewer parts, providing long and continual service.

When you purchase a burglar alarm system, regardless of the type or make, you will probably receive small stickers which are to be placed on windows and doors. These stickers state that your property is protected by a burglar alarm and usually give the name of the company producing or installing the equipment. The stickers are good since they may stop a burglar from even attempting to enter. But having the name of the company on the sticker is bad. This only tells the thief exactly what kind of system he is up against. If he is familiar with it, he may know to work around it. But if he does not know what kind of alarm he is facing, he may be afraid even to try. Therefore, if you use the stickers, first remove any company name with a razor blade as neatly as possible. There is no reason why you should tell the thief anything he should not know.

If you have a burglar alarm installed, use it! Probably half of those who do have alarms installed in their homes and businesses do not take the few seconds to turn them on when they leave.

3. Robbery

Robbery is the third least occurring crime in America, but it abbreviates the lives of more of its victims than any other crime against property. The sadness of these statistics is amplified by the fact that the loss of life as well as the robbery itself could, in 90 percent of the cases, have been avoided.

Business Robbery

Businesses which serve or sell food, liquor, and gasoline are the most frequent targets of robbers. However, any person, home, or business which handles or possesses large sums of cash, money orders, negotiable securities, and jewelry is a likely prospect. Ironic as it may seem, banks and other financial institutions (which handle the most money) account for less than 2 percent of the total number of robberies.

Eliminating flaws to make businesses secure from robbery is not always easy or possible. One of the country's finest security companies, Brinks Incorporated, learned this on the night of January 17, 1950 when eight masked gunmen robbed their Boston express office of $2,775,385.12.

Architectural design without security in mind, such as windowless buildings and placement of cashier stands where they cannot be easily seen from the outside, is one of the greatest aids to robbers. Floor plans are obviously not subject to change. But many steps can be taken to reduce the threat of robbery and insure the safety of employees and customers.

Advertisement signs on windows should be at least six feet from floor level. Never place displays in front of windows or around cashier stands. Robbers love businesses where the outside view is blocked, mainly because half of all robberies are reported by passersby.

The presence of security, real or artificial, will stop a robber better than anything. If the business is a large one such as a chain grocery store, a uniformed guard can be provided. Many companies use off-duty policemen as security guards, often out of uniform. This is a mistake. The robber, not recognizing the plainclothes officer, may proceed to rob the business. If the security officer then tries to stop the robbery, it can end in a shoot-out and innocent lives may be lost. The first duty of any security guard should be to prevent the crime from occurring. He can best do this by being obvious, not by hiding in a back room and waiting until a robbery actually takes place. His obvious presence may also cut down on shoplifting, offsetting the cost of his salary.

If there are many businesses together as in a shopping plaza or mall, a roving patrol can be formed and the expense shared by all parties.

An existing burglar alarm can also double as a robbery alarm for about twenty or thirty dollars by installing bypass switches on all windows and doors which remain open during business hours, and push-button type switches at all cashier stations and wherever money is kept. If the business has an office from which a robbery can be observed, a robbery alarm can also be placed there.

It is not, however, advisable to add robbery alarms to a nonsilent burglar alarm. The sudden sound of the loud alarm may cause a nervous robber to panic, go berserk, and start shooting wildly. It also may cause customers to stampede.

Push-button alarm switches should be located on the floor, or underneath a bottom edge near the floor where it can be pressed by raising the toe of the shoe against it, but never pressed by accident. *Never* place one where it can be pressed by hand, unless inside a safe. A robber will hurt you for pushing an alarm more quickly than for any other reason. The button must be out of sight and pressed unnoticed. *If you cannot press the alarm unnoticed, do not press it until the robber leaves.*

When placing a robbery alarm inside a safe, use a leaf-type switch. To set off the alarm, you only have to remove some object which is applying pressure to the switch; a cigar box, for instance. But be sure to use something which will not be moved accidentally and bring the police running to the business. Remember the story about the little boy who cried wolf once too often.

Cameras also can be attached to the alarm system to record a robbery on film and aid in the capture of the culprits. But the mere presence of a camera may deter a robber. No thief wants his picture taken.

There are other means of bringing security measures to the attention of the would-be robber. Place large, professionally printed signs on all doors and on the front of cashier stations stating that the business is protected by armed guards, silent alarms, and closed circuit television. These signs must be of high quality, lest they be ignored. The robber's greatest fear is being caught inside. He will avoid this possibility at all costs.

Many small businesses look upon security as a luxury instead of the necessity that it is. Often they refuse to invest in even the minimum requirements. But for as little as five dollars they can greatly reduce the chances of becoming targets. The signs discussed previously can be installed even if no other security measures are taken.

This will have the same discouraging effect as long as employees do not broadcast the fact they are contrived.

Phony surveillance cameras (about twenty dollars each) can also be used. As the business grows, real security can be added.

Fast food franchises, motels and other businesses who transact exclusively from one location such as windows and offices, find themselves facing the robber's gun far too often. The solution to this problem is not inexpensive.

A window and drawer of the type used by drive-in banks, complete with bulletproof glass, can be installed in one day for about $500. The drawer, of course, should be of adequate size to accommodate the merchandise sold, and a speaker system installed so orders can be taken with ease. High as the cost may seem, the unit should pay for itself in reduced insurance cost alone.

The presence of a large dog will generally help discourage robbery. But a robber with a gun will most likely shoot it. Local health officials should first be consulted since many locales have restrictions regarding animals in certain businesses.

The best routine a business can have for handling money and making deposits is *no routine at all.* Robbers are quick to pinpoint when and where the money will be, the number of personnel present, and so on. If daily operations–such as opening for business, distributing and counting money, breaking for lunch, and making deposits–are scheduled at different times (varied even by ten minutes either way), and by different people each day, it will be difficult for a robber to plan accurately.

Bank deposits can be made safely by an armored car company. Self-depositing is downright dangerous. Each year many people carrying bank deposits are ambushed, waylaid, and sniped. If deposits must be made by company personnel, the driver should never take the same route twice in succession, and should avoid all possible stop signs and red lights. These are notorious places for ambushes. Minor traffic accidents are also a favorite means of stopping a bank courier.

Home Robbery

Premeditated home robberies have surged astronomically in the past decade. Although these robberies are usually limited to middle- and upper-class homes, victims can include anyone harboring valuables where burglars cannot find them, or would have trouble obtaining them, such as in a safe.

The most desired method used by the home robber is to enter an unoccupied residence and wait for the owner to return. While he waits he will ransack the rooms in hopes of finding what he believes to be there. A robbery can be avoided at this point by observing the advice given in the chapter on burglary.

If the robber cannot gain access to the home by burglary, he will either force or trick his way into the house. And if you think a man cannot force his way into your home you are only deceiving yourself. A determined man with a thirty-pound sledge hammer can knock your door off its hinges, regardless of the locks.

The best way to see a door caller without being seen is to install a *one-way viewer* in all doors. This small device is about the size of your thumb, costs about two dollars, and will permit almost a full 180-degree view through the door without being seen. Installation takes about thirty minutes and requires only a half-inch hole drilled in the door at eye level.

The most common means of trick entry is to pose as a policeman (as in the 1968 Barbara Jane Mackle kidnapping case), telephone repairman (after first cutting the wires), delivery man, maintenance man (as in the infamous Boston Strangler rape-murders of the early 1960s), or a person in distress or needing to use a phone.

People will open their doors to a uniformed policeman, which is a mistake. Police uniforms can be bought at many stores without showing any identification, complete with insignias, stripes, badges, and identification cards. Policemen should not be allowed inside your home unless you are fully aware of their reason for being there or unless they have a warrant and show it to you. Even then you should first look for a patrol car. If a policeman claims to be bringing news of an accident or death in the family, confirm the information first by calling the police he claims to represent.

Any disruption of telephone service should be reported at once to the telephone company. As everyone who has ever had trouble with a telephone knows, a repairman will not suddenly appear. If a serviceman does call and you have not reported any trouble, even though you may then find your line to be dead, do not let him in. Telephone company uniforms can also be purchased easily, and trucks simply stolen.

Never accept a delivery unless you are aware of an order being placed, or without first calling the company to confirm the delivery. If the company cannot be reached you can have the delivery man leave the package outside. Wait until he leaves before opening the door and taking the package inside.

Repair or servicemen who visit on a regular basis, such as exterminators, should be known by sight. If not, the company should be called and asked to identify the employee.

Strangers, male or female, should never be permitted into a home, even if they give a reason. If they wish to make a telephone call, make it for them, but never permit them inside. Women are often used to gain entrance in home robberies.

The home robber is more apt to be professional than a business robber. He has somehow learned the routine of the family, what valuables are present and, possibly, where they are located. The only reason for a robbery is that the desired merchandise cannot be obtained through a burglary. Robbers are often very determined people with one-track minds. They are not easily discouraged from reaching their goal.

Standard procedure for the robbers is to gain entry, quickly and quietly if possible. They handcuff or tie their victims together in one room, taking whatever they came after. As long as they can find what they are looking for they will usually not harm anyone. But thieves have a bad habit of overestimating their prospective thefts. This can prove very painful for the home robbery victim.

Torturing victims to obtain the whereabouts of valuables by scalding with boiling water, breaking bones, and pulling out fingernails and teeth with pliers is more common than people wish to believe.

To help convince the robber you are telling the truth, you can offer to show him personal financial records, including bills of sale, and especially insurance papers which itemize insured possessions. A thief should understand that anything so valuable would surely be insured.

Push-button robbery alarms can be added to a home burglar alarm system for about four dollars per location. Unlike the store alarm, the home alarm need not be silent. The home robber is less prone to panic and will only want to escape the ear-piercing alarm.

If a robbery alarm is installed, a push-button type switch should be placed by every outside door. Bypass switches also can be placed by each door to permit entry without turning off the alarm system. The bypass switches are very important since the robber could trick his way into the home before announcing the robbery. In such a case the alarm would still be active and only the button need be touched to set off the alarm.

Push-button switches should also be placed in hallways leading to bedrooms, living rooms, and dens. These are the most likely places a robber will take his victim for holding and questioning.

Place the switches behind a picture frame or under a light switch, where they can be triggered by merely applying pressure to the frame or touching the switch without being noticed. There is also the possibility the robber will set off the alarm by accident or out of curiosity.

Additional switches can be placed on the edge of headboards, night stands, and end tables in bedrooms, living rooms, and dens. Here they can be pressed if the victims are tied up during or after the robbery.

Face to Face

When coming face to face with a robber, you are in the most dangerous position you will ever find yourself. You have no way of knowing whether or not the perpetrator has just buoyed his nerve with liquor, has scrambled his brains with LSD, is acting out of desperation to support a drug habit, or is stealing to prevent his family from becoming destitute.

Once you realize you are being robbed by an armed person, do not cry out, reach for a gun or other weapon, or try to fight him. These are the quickest ways to get hurt.

Do not try to be humorous or sarcastic by saying something like, "You've got to be kidding," or, "There it is, get it yourself." Many people have died uttering such phrases. People do not hold weapons on strangers and announce they are robbing them as a joke. If the robber wanted to get the money himself, he would have killed you and stepped over your body and got it. So to show you he is serious he may shoot or stab you, or at least put a few knots on your head.

You should always give the robber what he wants, do exactly as you are told, and move circumspectly. If you move too quickly, your action may seem accelerated, especially if the robber is drunk or on drugs. He may think you are reaching for a weapon or trying to escape. If you move too slowly, the robber may feel you are stalling for time. The end result in either instance could be fatal.

Remember, robbers are usually as scared as their victims and only want to get what they came after and get away as quickly as possible. The more problems you cause the robber, the fewer are your chances of coming out of the robbery alive.

If you are hit or wounded by a robber, fall down, remain silent and do not move. Don't even breathe if you can help it. This will make the robber's job easier and, hopefully, he will just take what he wants and leave. If you scream or call for help he may shoot or stab you, or beat you into unconsciousness.

The next subject is a touchy one—being kidnapped by a robber. The only reasons a robber will kidnap a victim, except for hostage-taking, are to rape or kill the victim. The robber is obviously afraid to rape or kill the victim at the scene of the crime or he would do so then and there. The only answer: don't go with him. Fainting is the simplest way out. Just fall down and stay down—no matter what. It will be difficult if not impossible for the robber to hold a weapon on you and carry you to his car at the same time. If he puts the weapon away, then you have a chance to fight, run, or scream. But you would be a fool to go willingly and unresistingly with him. You have absolutely nothing to lose by not going and everything to gain.

Never pursue a robber. If you can get a description of him, his car, and license number without being exposed to gunfire, by all means do so. If not, don't worry about it. Other people almost always see the getaway car. Because they are not the victims, they will be in a better mental state to describe it accurately to the police.

4. Con Games

Pyramid Selling

Pyramid selling is the largest and most successful con game in America today. During the last fifteen years a dozen or so of these companies have sprung up and hypnotized the success-seeking public. This con game has left many people distraught, disillusioned, broke, and with almost no recourse.

The sales pitch of the pyramid salesman is very simple and sounds very profitable, until considered in depth. These "opportunities" are usually presented at rallies which are organized through advertisements or acquaintances. The company's representative will claim to be seeking distributors of products ranging from mink oil and cosmetics to self-improvement courses. The products can be purchased or sold only by direct selling and will not be offered in stores, by mail order, or any other source. The distributorships cost from $1,000 to $3,500 and include sales training and a complete stock of company products which can be sold at 100 percent markup. Not only does being a distributor give the right to sell the company's product, but the right to sell other distributorships as well.

For every distributorship you sell to someone else, you receive a commission of about $200. Every time the new distributor purchases additional products, you again receive a commission. But not only will you receive a commission on other distributors' sales, but on every new distributorship they enlist to the company force, and the ones they enlist, and so on. In short, if you sell five distributorships and each of your distributors sell five, and each of theirs sell five, and so on, by the time the tenth rung of the ladder is reached, you have 1,953,125 distributors from which you receive a sales commission. This sounds wonderful—only you no longer have much of a consumer market.

Therefore, no one is actually selling the products, only distributorships. Since you receive a commission only on products which are reordered, after the commission for the distributorships you sold personally, you have no income. Your only options are to peddle from door to door the products you received when purchasing your distributorship, or to sell more distributorships for the commission.

The companies offer no buy-back guarantee against the sale of the products and the distributor is often stuck with a closet full of unusable products. The initial investment is unrecoverable and the company is not liable in many states. But there are some states which have recognized this great fraud and have passed laws to protect the unsuspecting public. Hopefully, some day all states will have laws prohibiting pyramid selling.

Improvements on the Home Front

Inferior home improvements constitute one of the oldest and most profitable con games. Businesses open overnight, operate until the proverbial walls start to close in, and vanish without a trace.

Springtime house painting is a yearly or biyearly occurrence in many homes. Most people believe that one painter is as good as another. They generally feel they cannot be defrauded if they personally select the brand of paint and the job is completed as proposed.

Even if the consumer selects the brand of paint, or buys the paint himself, it does not in any way insure that will in fact be the paint which covers the walls. Poor quality surplus paint can be bought for a song in fifty-gallon drums. Any desired brand of empty paint cans is available at the city dump or landfill, refillable with the low grade paint. By the time the paint begins to peel and flake away a month or two later, the painters have disappeared.

With wall-to-wall carpeting came the *crooked carpet layers.* Carpets are items which are expected to last from seven to nine years, and should be selected with the greatest of care. Choose those who install them with equal care.

The first thing to remember is there are many fine companies with dishonest employees. It is impossible for the larger companies to inspect every job, making sure their employees carry out orders without substituting a lower grade of carpet. Do not select a company by name alone, and do not forget a follow-up check of the merchandise.

Calculate the correct square yardage of carpet you will need; multiply the length by the breadth of each room and divide the total number of feet by nine. Do not depend on the company for an accurate measurement. You may find yourself paying for nonexistent carpet and installation.

If you know little about carpet, you should first select the color, pattern, and type of carpet. Then obtain a swatch of your selection and take it to several other manufacturers and outlets for an appraisal of quality and price. This will also give you competitive pricing which can save you hundreds of dollars.

When you have decided on the carpet and installation company, have *all* information, including the name brand, manufacturer's model number, style, cost per yard, and guarantee *written* into the contract. If the company has no contract, beware.

At the time of installation, someone well versed in carpet should be present to verify you are getting exactly what you are paying for.

Pest exterminators are not really what their name implies. Pest *controllers* would be the proper name. It has never been the intention of the exterminators to completely eliminate the insect population of a home or business. Doing so would eventually literally work them out of a job.

Therefore when you consider having your property treated against insects, whether they be termites or roaches, exercise caution when reading and signing contracts. You may find yourself signing up for a five- to ten-year program complete with hidden yearly costs for monthly visits. If you sell your property, many contracts hold you liable for continued treatments and payments.

Many companies have a bad habit of initially exaggerating the extent of damages and the need for services. Always get at least three complete estimates before making a decision and signing a contract. If you let the companies know you are making multiple inquiries they may lower their estimates substantially.

Many pests can be controlled by regular, weekly, self-sprayings around woodwork, cabinets, attics, basements, and garages. It is best to first try halting any pest problems yourself. If no change is seen after a month or so, a pest control expert should be consulted. But many pest problems can be solved without professional aid.

Prior to purchasing any property or real estate, old or new, be sure to have it inspected for insects. If a problem is detected, the present owner should correct it.

Hit-and-run roofing and driveway firms are infamous

in the home improvement business. They usually confront the homeowner with the offer of making his home into the "showplace of the neighborhood," a "model" to attract other business for a small but growing company. For only the cost of materials, they will say, the old cracked and leaking shingle roof will be removed and a new fiberglass or slate roof installed. The uneven gravel or dirt driveway will be graded and blacktopped with asphalt. As icing on the cake, twenty-five dollars is promised to the homeowner for every new customer who comes to the company as a result of the "model."

Before the work can begin, however, the owner is asked to make a downpayment, or even to pay in full. Once this is accomplished, the company usually disappears. With fifty to one hundred "showplace" projects climaxing at the same time, the company makes a tidy profit.

If the company feels it can make a greater profit by completing the work, it will install a new roof of pressed cardboard and cover the driveway with a thin layer of asphalt. Of course after the first few rains and hot days, the roof is leaking all over the house and the driveway looks like a disaster area. But the company who did the work has completed all of its projects and is opening new offices in a distant city.

Insulation fraud—Thanks to the 1975 Arab oil embargo, Americans have become acutely aware that energy is not to be wasted. The result has touched each of us in a way never before experienced. One awareness, which no one will dispute, is that well-insulated homes save energy, and therefore save money for those who must pay for it.

President Carter tried to encourage homeowners and businesses to conserve energy by promising to rebate in taxes 20 to 30 percent of the cost of insulating and using alternate sources of energy. Unfortunately, the proposal became bogged down in committees and was not approved in time for taxpayers to receive relief on their 1977 returns, but has been available since then.

Where there is great demand for a product, there also will be some fraud. Already there are cries to Congress for regulation of the quality and production of insulation and other energy-saving products. But until this needed proposal can find its way through the maze of bureaucratic committees and red tape, one must be very careful selecting insulation, specifically, and all energy-saving devices in general.

When buying insulation the main point of concern should be the *R factor,* which by law must appear on each piece or roll of blanket insulation and on containers of loose insulation. The *R factor* indicates the ability of the insulation to withstand heat and cold. The higher the number following the *R* the greater the insulating ability.

But there is another point of concern of equal importance. This is the fireproof quality of the product. Supposedly, all insulation is fire-resistant, if not fireproof. This feature requires special treatment which many small firms do not employ. Always perform the simple test of holding a lighted match to a small piece of the material to see if, or how quickly, it will burn. Loose insulation seems to be the most flammable.

Never buy insulation from door-to-door salesmen. Although the price may be attractive, you will pay for it many times over in increased heating and cooling cost.

Use the same procedure when purchasing insulation as with any other home improvement products: know what you are buying and compare prices and quality.

Better Business Bureau

The Better Business Bureau is the best friend a homeowner can have when searching for reliable service and merchandise. The consumer service can tell you if there has ever been a complaint made against a company or a product, and how long the company has been in business. The Better Business Bureau can also recommend an established and reliable company to perform the work, but cannot insure against fraud by the companies or their employees. It is always best to double-check and compare when possible. The best check one can make is to ask for several references and make inquiries regarding satisfaction.

Short-Changing

Every year thousands of good, honest employees are dismissed from their jobs with blemished work records because of the short-change artist. Since employers themselves are unaware of the operational methods of the flim-flam man, they assume the employees have willfully taken the money, instead of having it unknowingly taken from them. The employee will be fired and "stealing" entered into the work record as grounds for dismissal. Needless to say, this has a devastating effect when seeking new employment.

The flim-flam man is indeed an artist. His manner of dress is correspondent with the surroundings, his speech is explicit and confident, and his performance is presented with Oscar perfection. Even if he is detected, deception is all but impossible to prove.

The victims are selected according to their actions while working. Women are selected more often by men and men are selected more often by women flim-flam artists. One who is timid, nervous, self-conscious, easily excited, of inferior intelligence, or very busy, is more likely to be selected.

Although the denomination of the currency involved in the short-change operation may vary with the confidence of the perpetrator, the methods change very little. The most common operation employs the use of a twenty-dollar bill and a one-dollar bill. The con artist comes to the cashier and makes a purchase totaling exactly one dollar including taxes. As payment he or she will present a twenty-dollar bill, all the while talking in a soothing voice about some disarming subject.

The cashier will normally give one ten-dollar bill, one five-dollar bill, and four one-dollar bills as change for the twenty-dollar bill presented for the one-dollar purchase.

When the flim-flam artist is handed the change, he will ask, "What is this for?"

The cashier, of course, will explain the change is for the twenty-dollar bill given to pay for the purchase.

The artist will look surprised, then check inside his wallet and find a one-dollar bill. "I'm sorry," he will say, counting the money repeatedly from one hand to the other, "I meant to give you this one-dollar bill. I don't really need all these small bills."

The artist will then count out five one-dollar bills and the one five-dollar bill where the cashier can see them. "Here," he will say, gesturing toward the cash register. "Let me give you this five and five ones, and you can give me a ten." Then he will immediately look down and begin counting the money over and over, all the while talking about the small bills he doesn't need, until the cashier hands him the ten-dollar bill. At this time he will hand the cashier the five-dollar bill and four one-dollar bills instead of the five and five ones he had been counting.

By force of habit the cashier will probably count the money before putting it into the cash register and should catch the mistake. In fact, the con artist *wants* the cashier to catch the mistake.

In the meantime the artist has slipped the ten-dollar bill into his pocket and waits for the cashier to make the next move.

If the cashier catches the mistake he or she will say, "But you only gave me a five and four ones."

The artist is shocked and asks, "Are you sure? Let me see."

The cashier will then count the money out in front of him. The artist in turn picks up the bills and adds a ten-dollar bill and another one-dollar bill. Mixing the money together he will then count the money back to the cashier, laying down the five-dollar bill first, the ten-dollar bill next, and the five one-dollar bills last, saying, "Here. Five, fifteen, sixteen, seventeen, eighteen, nineteen, twenty." He is careful not to say the word "ten" and now holds up his empty hands to show he has no more money and adds, "Just give me my twenty-dollar bill back."

Ninety-nine percent of the time the cashier will completely forget about the ten dollars given for the five and five ones. Therefore the cashier will recount the ten, five, and five one-dollar bills and give the artist a twenty in return.

The short-change artist will leave with a twenty and a ten-dollar bill, and the purchase made for a dollar. He makes nine dollars and the dollar purchase as profit for the one-minute performance. If the con man makes fifteen short-changes per day, five days a week, in a year he will make $39,000—far more than some attorneys and college professors.

The key to the system lies in the cashier giving the artist the ten-dollar bill at the same time the crook gives the cashier the five and four ones. Although the cashier is violating the first rules he should learn—never give change until the exchange money has been counted and put into the cash register—too often he does so when caught off guard.

If the cashier makes the first mistake of giving the ten-dollar bill before receiving the five and four ones, but catches the attempt to keep the ten-dollar bill, and exchange the other ten, five and five ones for the twenty-dollar bill, the con artist will deny receiving the ten-dollar bill. But if the cashier steadfastly refuses to give the twenty-dollar bill in exchange, and threatens to call the police, the con artist will usually "find" the other ten-dollar bill, apologize, and try to laugh it off as an honest mistake.

The "serial number" short-change method is relatively old, requires two people, and never goes without confrontation, which is why it is not as common as the regular short-change method.

The artists first go to the bank and purchase a supply of new twenty-dollar bills with consecutive serial numbers. They will then select a cashier and one of the artists will make a small purchase, paying with one of the new twenty-dollar bills, receive his change and leave.

Next will come the second con man with the remainder of the new twenty-dollar bills. He makes a small purchase such as a pack of cigarettes with a dollar bill and waits for his change. When the cashier tries to give him change for the one-dollar bill, he will claim to have paid with a twenty-dollar bill.

Of course the cashier will rightfully argue that he was given only a one-dollar bill. The con man will then suggest that the manager be called and the cashier will agree.

By the time the manager arrives the con man has become highly indignant and the other customers waiting in line are getting impatient. The situation is quickly exlained and the manager sides with the cashier. Just as the battle appears to be won by the establishment, the con artist "remembers" that he has nothing but new twenty-dollar bills in his possession and they all have consecutive serial numbers. A quick check proves that the top twenty-dollar bill in the register has a serial number which is in sequence with the twenty-dollar bills in the possession of the artist. The store reluctantly pays off and the con man leaves, nineteen dollars richer.

If confronted with this kind of situation, the manager should call the police. They are well aware of this type of trickery and will not side with the con artist. Even the mention of calling the police will send con men scurrying away.

Coin Change

Until 1970, short-changing with coins seemed impractical and unprofitable. But an ex-convict from Atlanta, Georgia changed this assumption when he formulated and executed a system which caused banks and businesses throughout the country to change their methods of receiving coinage.

The ex-con bought and rebuilt a small punchpress, made a punch and die set exactly the same size as a quarter, picked up some scrap sixteen-gauge steel (almost exactly the same thickness as a quarter), sheared the scrap into one-inch strips, and proceeded to stamp out half a million perfect quarter slugs.

Then he rolled them into bank wrappers with a real quarter on each end to give the exact appearance, size, and weight of a ten-dollar roll of quarters.

He made his first appearance in the Florida panhandle. By visiting banks with real rolls of quarters, complete with the name and address of a well-known business, printed with a rubber stamp, he learned which bank tellers and drive-in window tellers would accept the rolls without opening them for inspection.

Early the next morning he returned to one teller and one drive-in window at each of the ten banks he had selected. At each he left behind slug-filled rolls. In less than an hour he had collected $5,000 and disappeared. By the time he was captured ten months later, after a teller dropped two of the phony rolls while he was still in the bank, he was cashing in fifty rolls at each teller and drive–in window at twenty banks, for a total take of $20,000 per city.

The moral of this story is never accept rolled coins without first checking to insure you are actually getting what you expect. Merely looking at the ends is not enough.

Funny Money

Three million dollars in counterfeit currency were dumped into the American economy last year. Another $32 million worth was seized before it could be circulated. Some of the phony money was of such high quality that it may float for years before it is detected.

Counterfeit money is almost without exception in ten- and twenty-dollar denominations. Smaller bills are unprofitable, since the objective is to make as small a purchase as possible with a large bill and receive the maximum amount of change in good currency. Bills larger than twenties tend to attract unwanted attention.

When a phony bill is detected, usually when it is deposited at the bank, it is turned over to the Secret Service. The lone loser is the person who accepted, but failed to detect, the phony bill. The bank will not give credit to the person who turned in the bill. Even if the holder of the counterfeit money can remember who they received the money from, it would be very difficult to prove its origin.

There is hope, however, for the business willing to invest about thirty dollars. A small counterfeit bill detector is now on the market. It requires no special installation and checks all currency by means of a special light, ringing a buzzer upon detection.

The best and easiest check is to look closely at the bill for the red and blue fibers which appear in all genuine U.S. currency. Also, look for lines which are not sharp and clear.

Bad and Bogus Checks

Counterfeit, stolen, and bad checks cost businesses millions of dollars each year, yet few take any real preventive action. The only explanation, if it can be called that, is that the lust for money supersedes all sense of caution.

Businesses that will not even consider cashing a check for someone personally known, will reverse the policy if the person makes only a minor purchase. Even banks cash checks for a stranger without requiring identification, if the person fills out a deposit slip for a few dollars to be placed in an account, and never confirm the account.

Photographically recording the check and its casher is a great deterrent. Since most thieves do not want their picture taken, they will avoid establishments who employ this method. But, it must be pointed out that the camera will have little effect upon the out-of-towner, or the person unknown to local police. Most police departments do not exchange mug shots. Therefore the photographs on file in one city may not be recorded in another only a few miles away.

The safest and surest method of discouraging and detecting the "paper hanger" is the one overlooked most often. Fingerprints are the ultimate tracers. And a thief will *never* willingly submit to having his fingerprints taken.

An ink pad can be used to coat the ends of the fingers and the impressions left on the back of the check. However, the last joint of all ten fingers must be recorded on the check. Contrary to beliefs, an identification cannot be obtained from a single fingerprint or thumb print. One print, however, can sustain the evidence and identity if the person is already known.

Identification papers such as driver's licenses, social

security cards, draft cards, student and business cards should never be considered as sufficient identification for cashing checks. All of these can easily be printed and sealed in plastic to resemble legitimate identification.

Diplomatically worded signs stating that due to company regulations, all unknown persons must submit to being photographed and fingerprinted will discourage more phony and bad check cashers. These signs will save the business more money than the few dollars which may be lost from those honest people who will not submit.

One other simple method of check protection, of course, is to call the bank on which the check is drawn to verify the account and assure its balance will cover the amount of the check. But remember, the bank does not deduct the amount of the check you called on until the check actually arrives at the bank. There is nothing stopping the check writer from writing dozens of checks on a small account and leaving town before the checks reach the bank. So unless you are reasonably sure of the check writer, do not let a telephone call to the bank be the sole caution against cashing a check.

If you are in doubt about a company check, call the company. Many payroll checks are stolen or counterfeited and sold to professional check cashers. Company identification cards, complete with pictures, are as easy to produce as the checks.

Take note that more females participate in crimes of deception (responsible for one-third of the total) than in any other kind of crime. Their roles are not secondary and they should be regarded with equal prudence.

5. Shoplifting

Shoplifting, or *boosting* as it is often called, attracts more individuals from a greater variety of lifestyles than any other crime. Shoplifting is often forgotten, however, until the name of a Hollywood starlet, professional athlete, political personality, novelist, or otherwise famous person makes the headlines for shoplifting some trifling, inexpensive item. Even then it is only with amusement we view this serious crime which increases inflation more than all other crimes combined.

Most crimes against property such as robbery and burglary are at least covered in part by insurance. The crime rate, obviously, does have a direct effect upon insurance premiums. But the over $5 billion lost each year through shoplifting is not covered by insurance. Since no company can afford such a loss, the adjustment is made in the pricing of each item. Losses are passed on to the consumer in the form of higher prices.

The theft of an item of necessity by a destitute person for a needy family is understandable. Not justifiable, but understandable. But why individuals who literally own fortunes will shoplift unimportant items is beyond comprehension. Perhaps they are feeding an ego craving for the risk and excitement connected with crime, without believing themselves to be criminal. Or, the individuals may be able to see their behavior as more or less justified under the "everybody's doing it" cliche, either by a pathological twisting of reality or by the more ordinary defenses that they erect around a valued picture of themselves.

But is not someone who unlawfully participates in causing the rising of inflation by billions of dollars each year as much a criminal as the common burglar or robber? This author fails to discern the difference.

In most states the crime of shoplifting is a misdemeanor. Punishment ranges from a few dollars' fine to a maximum of one year in jail, the latter being the extreme exception reserved for the professional shoplifter.

The relatively light punishment for even professional boosters has subsequently attracted other kinds of thieves into the shoplifting business. Like all professional thieves, they quickly adapt and learn the safest ways to steal merchandise.

There are many methods the professional booster uses to lift merchandise, including false, expanded, or hidden pockets in oversize coats. But this is old hat for modern boosters who know it is a sure ticket to jail if caught with merchandise on their persons. In fact, boosters have now changed the shoplifting game so radically that it is more of a con game than what one usually thinks of as shoplifting.

The most common method is for the booster to select a large, yet inexpensive item such as a plastic toy or garbage can, which is sealed and the cashier is not likely to open. In the case of a plastic toy, for instance, the booster will remove the toy from the box, stuff it with the desired merchandise (pants, shirts, shoes, etc.) and reseal the box. When he reaches the cashier station he will pay for the merchandise which is supposed to be in the box.

If for some reason the cashier opens the box and discovers the merchandise, the booster will claim he knew nothing about it. Since there is no proof he did know, unless someone saw him put the merchandise into the box, the store does not have a case which would stand up in court.

Surprisingly, only one cashier in ten will open sealed merchandise to check for the proper product. The solution is very simple. Open all containers, sealed or unsealed, and check the contents against the label on the box. In the case of large containers such as garbage cans, always look inside. It is not unusual for a booster to fill a garbage can full of merchandise and wire it shut so the cashier will have difficulty getting it open, and therefore pass it over.

Boosting in Booths

Putting on new clothes under old ones in try-on booths costs clothing stores plenty. This quick-change artistry can occur only if a shopper is allowed to carry several articles into the booth at once. To prevent this kind of theft the management need only keep the booths locked. Require a salesperson to unlock the booth and assure the customer does not take but one article of clothing into the booth at a time, and that it be returned before another is tried on.

Shoe Switching

The old shoe switch trick is as common as rain, especially in self-service stores. The booster will walk in wearing an old pair of shoes, purchased at a second-hand store for about fifty cents, with a small tin of mud in his pocket. At first opportunity he will smear mud on a pair of expensive shoes to make them appear old, exchange the shoes he wore into the store for the new pair, and stroll out of the store.

The shoe switch, however, is not limited to the professional booster. Housewives, students, and others who simply do not have the money to buy shoes use this method.

The only answer to this problem is good, alert employees. But there is one distinct, easily recognized characteristic which almost all shoe switchers share: they never want direct assistance, although they may ask where a certain style is located. If the store is an easy mark, they will return again and again, but never make a purchase.

Price Changing

Price tag changing is just another form of shoplifting. Again, alert employees must be relied on for detection. Although it is virtually impossible to memorize the price of every item in even a small store, there are a few mistakes price changers make which can easily be spotted.

Store employees who attach price tags tend to form an easily remembered pattern. One may place the price tags on the second button of all shirts. Another may place the tags in a certain place on the right leg of all pants. Since the price switcher is very seldom a professional thief, he is not likely to notice such a small detail and will consequently place the new price tag in another location. In his haste, he may place the tag crooked or even upside down. An alert cashier will catch many price changes by this system every day.

Price stickers such as those used on boxes, cannot be easily removed without being damaged. Even if they are, they cannot be placed over the original sticker without leaving a telling edge protruding. Alert cashiers should look for signs of torn or overlapping stickers, or boxes with raw places where a sticker could have been removed.

Use of Mirrors

Round convex mirrors are good deterrents and detectors of shoplifters. Placed at a height just above the counter tops and tilted slightly downward, the mirrors can be adjusted to give the desired observation.

Full-length mirrors serve a dual purpose. Not only will they permit total observation, but will allow shoppers to see themselves as well. No one wants to look into a mirror and see himself stealing. If a thief can see himself stealing, he feels someone else can also see him.

Confronting the Shoplifter

If a shoplifter is observed, *never* attempt to apprehend him. This is a job for police or security personnel. Not all shoplifters are particularly gentle people. The most diplomatic method would be to confront the person at the check-out station and quietly ask if he would like to pay for the articles or objects pocketed, or would he prefer you notify the police. Reluctantly he will pay, if he is able to do so.

Names and addresses should be taken from shoplifters and given to the management. Many companies keep files on shoplifters and will permit a first offender to get by with only a warning. Often, this will cure any desires a person has of pocketing goods without giving him a criminal record. But if his name turns up a second time he should be turned over to the police.

Should a confronted shoplifter refuse to cooperate or even give his name, get a good description of the person and the car if possible and give it to the police. Do not try to make the arrest yourself unless you are qualified.

6. Murder

Everyone has his own definition of the most serious crime. Some will undoubtedly say the trafficking of narcotics, piracy of an aircraft, or treason. Many will select kidnapping for ransom, or rape. And still others will view an assault which leaves the victim a paraplegic, or otherwise permanently disabled, as unsurpassed.

But how can there be any greater crime than the unlawful taking of a human life? To remove, by the squeezing of a trigger or the thrust of a knife, a person from his family and loved ones, forever. Does not the act of murder leave more victims in its aftermath than the act itself, or that of any other crime?

Yes, murder is indeed the ultimate crime. Although it is feared above all others, when it is faced, we refuse to discuss it or take any action to prevent our lives from being snuffed out like a candle flame in a sudden breeze. Even those who do dare think of this crime feel there is nothing they can do to prevent it.

Prevention *is* possible. Three-fourths of the murders committed in the United States each year are not premeditated. They are committed by people in acts of rage or passion. Most often murderers are influenced by alcohol and/or faced with an emotional crisis.

We may not like to admit it, but the potential to be this kind of murderer exists in almost everyone. Can we truly say what we would do if faced with a jolting scene like finding our spouse or lover in bed with another person?

It must be remembered that the majority of murderers has never committed a criminal act; the murder was the first crime.

Literature has made us think of murder in a far different sense. Premeditated murder is the favorite topic of the mystery novel. Therefore, despite its actual low incidence, felonious homicide remains the supposedly archetypal murder. Even Cain's slaying of Abel has been reenacted and interpreted with endless fascination. The murderers who emerge in literature are of great variety: the woman who slowly poisons her husband to death with a mysterious South American herb to collect his insurance; the paid underworld assassin who kills in cold blood; the terrorist who uses murder as a political gesture; the man who plans the perfect destruction of another as an act of self-definition; the sadistic madman who vents his rage against the world; the sadomasochistic murderer of children who dismembers his victims; and the schoolboy who kills a casually selected victim on an idle dare. Unquestionably such murders do in fact occur. But the great mass of homicides committed in the United States each year is far more pedestrian, far less dramatic in motivations and methods.

The pangs of jealousy; the accumulations of hostility generated in arguments; the indignity of humiliating public exploits; the wounding of the ego—all may create a situation in which the individual may strike back at the person he feels is the provoker. The act of aggression is mainly a form of retaliation.

Physical aggression without anger or hate is, therefore, relatively rare, and the cold-blooded killer, the happy brawler, or the ideological murderer is more common in fiction than in mundane reality, although he does exist.

Measures Against Murder

Operating within each of us are needs, drives, and motives that impel us to act. Counteracting these are both internal and external emotional and social controls that modify, inhibit, and harness the forces. When hostilities accumulate to an unbearable degree, we are pushed headlong over the barriers imposed by self and society.

The environment in which each of us was reared and now resides has a great bearing on what we can endure without physical retaliation. In some cultures a blow of the fist is accepted as casually as a tongue-lashing. In other social classes such an act would be unthinkable and possibly result in the death of the striker.

Intra-family murders usually occur as the climax of an uncontrollable emotional reaction and are rapidly regretted. Therefore the availability of a weapon, usually a handgun or knife, may determine the outcome of such an outburst. Many murders have been committed by individuals grabbing and using a weapon before realizing the course of their actions or considering the results. If the weapon had not been available, the critical moment may well have passed without injury or death inflicted.

A family which has violent quarrels, or a member who is prone to destructive impulses, should take precautionary action to insure no weapon is readily available at any time.

Knives should be locked in a strong cabinet or drawer and the keys kept in an opposite part of the house.

Guns should be kept unloaded and ammunition placed in separate rooms under lock and key.

During the few minutes it will take a person to obtain a weapon not readily available, he is likely to bring his emotions under control. This prevention also has a second effect no less important. These extra few minutes may allow prospective victims to escape safely.

It is also not advisable to go to sleep after a heated argument if all issues are not settled. Murdering a sleeping person is not uncommon, especially by the more cowardly types. Therefore it is always best to talk through problems thoroughly, leaving no trace of animosity to erupt later that night.

People do not believe they are going to be murdered until, perhaps, those last few moments before their lives are abbreviated. They think their sometimes violent but loving spouse, lover, or family member could never take their lives. Therefore it is difficult to accept advice at face value.

There are, however, at least 36,000 people who would have or do wish they had talked out their problems, removed the availability of weapons, been faithful to their husbands and wives, or sought psychiatric or alcoholic counseling to find solutions to their emotional and drinking problems. Nineteen thousand of these people were killed via family quarrels last year; 17,000 went to prison for taking those lives. All statistics are testimonials to the fact that violence has become a dangerous and familiar companion.

7. Rape

During 1979, rape increased 13.2 percent throughout the United States; an estimated total of 75,989 cases were reported; probably more than 500,000 incidents went unreported. Since 1975, rape has increased 35 percent, while arrests for that crime are up only 14 percent. Rape is the fastest growing, least reported, second most apprehendable, yet least convictable crime today.

Rape is indeed the second most serious of all crimes, yielding only to murder. It is the crime in which the victim will suffer the greatest psychological damage, it is feared above all other crimes, and yet is least prepared for. It is a crime which must be curbed.

In New York City, Chicago, Atlanta, Detroit, and in the District of Columbia and other places, special clinics, analytic units, and prevention centers have been organized to handle rape cases. Many other cities have one or more of these in their planning and development programs. A bill has been introduced in Congress to set up a National Center for Control and Prevention of Rape, in hopes of altering many of the present laws which are overbalanced in favor of the perpetrator.

We must have laws to guard against false accusations—of the scared teen-ager who cries rape when caught in the act of willful intercourse; or of a jealous, jilted, or otherwise infuriated woman. Such cases do exists and in no small numbers. If some precautions were not taken, wrongful convictions could ruin the reputations and lives of innocent men.

However, the guidelines for obtaining convictions under present law are often so strict that corroborating physical and medical evidence is not sufficient to sustain a conviction. Some states even require eyewitnesses to support the victim's testimony. The burden of proof is shifted to the victim.

This leaves us only to gaze in wonderment at our present judicial system which is harboring, however unintentionally, these sick and vicious people. Our state lawmakers must also share the blame. If they continue to refuse to take legislative action, they should undoubtedly be remembered at reelection time.

Portrait of a Victim

According to predictions based on yearly increases, between 1,100 and 1,400 of every 100,000 women in cities with populations of 250,000 or more will be raped this year. Of these, only about one-third will report the crime to authorities.

Women who live in suburban or rural areas are 3.5 times less likely to be raped than those who live in large cities.

The most common place and time for a rape to occur is in or near the victim's or attacker's residence, between dark and 3 A.M. Incidence in parking lots, automobiles, alleys, parks, elevators, and college dormitories follow respectively.

Almost all victims are under the age of twenty-five, with the average being about twenty.

Following a present-day rape case from the commission of the act to disposition is a trying experience for anyone. The victim first must notify the police. If the rape occurred away from home, the victim may wait until she reaches either her own residence or that of a friend before doing so. However, she must account for leaving the scene.

If she changes her clothes, takes a bath, applies fresh make-up, or even rearranges her hair before investigating officers arrive, she will be frowned upon for tampering with evidence.

To add to the victim's mental torment, the investigators are usually regular patrolmen whose personalities have been seasoned by years of arresting drunks and prostitutes and who possess neither the patience nor the training to deal tactfully with the situation.

The victim is then taken to a hospital where she must wait in the hustle and bustle of a crowded waiting room until she can be seen. Eventually, an intern or nurse who probably has no special training in handling rape cases will examine the victim to determine the extent of physical damage. Besides the treatment of any wounds which may have been received, evidence is collected. Bruises on arms, legs, and body are photographed. The vagina is examined for forced entry and sperm. (In many states if there is no sperm, rape cannot be sustained.) Before leaving the hospital the victim is given an appointment to return within five days to be examined for venereal disease and asked for her address so *she* can be sent a bill for services rendered.

If and when the attacker is arrested, the victim not only must positively identify him, but must repeat the entire story to investigators from the prosecutor's office as well as the grand jury. This part of the judicial system, however, has not been and should not be changed. To do so would be to deny equal rights and protection allotted to any and all accused persons.

By now the victim is somewhat pessimistic about the prospect of her attacker being convicted. That discouragement partially explains why 30 percent of the victims do not appear for the trial. Consequently, the rapist goes free.

There is another reason why victims do not appear for court. Often, they realize that they, too, are as much on trial as the suspect. Each victim is questioned in open court by the suspect's attorney about every aspect of her personal life. What was she doing out at night alone? Or, if the attack occurred at her home, did she undress without closing the draperies? What kind of clothing was she wearing at the time of the attack? Were the clothes tight, sexy, or short? Was she trying to pick up a man? Has she ever picked up a man? Has a man ever picked her up? If any of these questions are not answered to the satisfaction of the attorney, their meaning is twisted into a leading act on the part of the victim.

When questioning is directed to the attack itself, an effort is often made to slander the victim. Why didn't she call for help when attacked? (If no one heard her cries, it is assumed she did not make a noise.) Was she drinking? Was she physically and mentally capable of defending herself? If so, why didn't she? (Many cases have been thrown out because the judge or the jury felt the victim did not strenuously resist the attacker.) Was she wearing a bra and panties? (If not, she is considered a "bad girl" and it is generally assumed a bad girl can't be raped.) Did she or the attacker remove her clothes? (If she did, she was not resisting enough.) Was she a virgin at the time of the attack? If not, and not married, how many men has she had intercourse with? How often, married or not? Had she ever been unfaithful to her husband? Did she know the attacker? If yes, did she ever willingly have intercourse with him? And if so, how often?

In what position was she raped? How long did the rape last? Did she ask the attacker to stop? (If not, she did not resist enough.) Did she enjoy it? Did the attacker have a climax? Did she have a climax? (If yes, she enjoyed it.) Did she perform sodomy on the attacker or him on her? Did she enjoy it?

These examples of questions are not by any means exaggerations. In fact, they are mild by many courtroom standards. Rape is an emotionally terrifying, as well as physically damaging, ordeal for any woman to suffer. But the treatment she receives in the aftermath of the attack is another crime in itself.

It is not such a complex or expensive problem to establish an ideal postrape system to aid the victim in this trying time. Police officers–preferably policewomen–can be trained to respond, diplomatically question, and console the rape victim. Immediately afterwards is the time the victim needs compassionate, experienced guidance, not some burly traffic patrolman with a flair for insults and insinuations.

One efficient nurse or female intern, hand-picked and trained to gently handle the rape victim, should be on duty in every hospital at all times. The hospital should also provide a special area separating the rape victim from the regular hospital traffic. The treatment of these victims in the first few hours is crucial to their psychological as well as physical recovery. The investigative and medical teams hold this key.

These services need only be redesigned within the already established departments and agencies. Revamping legislation is another matter. The laws which allow the exploitation of a rape victim before a court of law, subjecting her to the worst kind of harassment and humiliation by permitting immaterial and irrelevant questioning and character destruction, must be repealed. Many state legislators have already begun to repeal or change the necessary laws, but too many others have not. In the latter case, the public must let its views be known to state lawmakers. State laws can be changed, but often the public must take the first step.

Portrait of a Rapist

The typical rapist is between fourteen and twenty-six years old. He is a social and educational dropout, unmarried, and unable to hold a job. But rapists come in *all* shapes and sizes, and regardless of their status and attitudes, all rapists have one thing in common; they are mentally sick. Rape is the only crime which is not committed for profit, to aid the perpetrator's escape, prevent identification, or as a result of an argument.

Rapists are usually shy, paranoid, habitual liars who suffer from an inferiority complex due to repetitious rejections by the opposite sex. If they are ex-convicts at the time of the attack, they were probably homosexuals while in prison, either by choice or as the result of force by stronger inmates. The chances of their falling into the role of a homosexual when they return to prison is almost certain.

The fact that rapists are placed in institutions with ordinary criminals is a mistake in itself. These people are mentally ill and should be treated in maximum security psychiatric institutions exclusively for sex offenders.

Since the beginning of time, rape, and the punishment thereof, has been an issue of controversy among lawmakers as well as the general public. In ancient times, rape was punishable by putting out the eyes, castration, or both. As recently as June 27, 1972 when the United States Supreme Court struck down capital punishment in a landmark decision, twenty-six states still had laws on the books allowing the execution of rapists. This was especially true in cases involving interracial rapes, as 10 percent constitute.

All of these punishments were administered in the name of law and order with cries of their being deterrents. They were in fact deterrents, but only in the sense of stopping recividivism.

But how can you deter a disease? Would a man who has been bitten by a rabid skunk be put to death to protect himself and society without attempting to cure him? Certainly not! He would be admitted to the hospital which could best treat him and remain there until cured. Why then shouldn't a rapist be treated as the sick and deranged person he is, placed in an institution designed to protect society by preventing escape, until such time when he could be released without any doubt as to his mental stability.

The length of time a rapist remains in confinement and under treatment should depend entirely on the individual and the progress made toward restoring him to sane and useful citizenship. The term should *not* be determined by a sentence imposed by a judge or jury, or bargained for through the district attorney's office.

If a rapist is sentenced to five years' imprisonment, he may well emerge at the end of his sentence in equal or worse mental condition than at the time of his crime. In addition to being a rapist, he may become a burglar, robber, or murderer as well. Surely some rapists should never be returned to society. Psychiatric treatment will not help these few. They can prove helpful, however, in studying, researching, finding the causes of and, hopefully, a cure for this most proliferating and dreaded crime.

Attack Avoidance

Whenever a prospective rape victim faces an attacker, she faces a terrible dilemma. It may not always be possible for her to guard both her body and her life. There is no guideline defining what degree of physical resistance can safely be taken against an attacker. This should depend entirely upon the individual situation and the physical ability and condition of the victim. There are, however, many preventive measures which women can take.

When returning to an empty house, always look for signs of forced entry. If any are noticed, leave quickly and quietly. Go to the nearest telephone and call police.

Do not open doors to unknown persons, especially delivery men, salesmen, and repairmen. These are the most common guises used to enter an occupied residence for the purpose of rape. In nine of the thirteen infamous Boston Strangler rape-murders in the early sixties, the women opened their doors to a man masquerading as a repairman.

Homes equipped with burglar alarms should also include push-button robbery alarms by all outside doors (as described in the chapters on robbery and burglary).

All parking lots should be regarded with caution. They are favorite places for rapists to lurk.

Before entering an automobile, always check for persons hiding inside. If someone is inside, run and call for help as loudly as possible. It will take the person time to get out of the car and even if he does chase you, which is highly unlikely, you stand a better chance of survival in an open parking area than in a closed automobile.

When walking alone, always face the traffic. If a man tries to pick you up or force you into his car, you will be running away from the direction in which he is heading, or at least on the opposite side of the street. If faced with this situation, run for the nearest lighted or inhabited area. Do not remain on the same street if possible. This will only give the man a chance to rearrange his thoughts and make another attempt to pick you up. But do not change routes if doing so would place you in a less protected area.

The best protection a woman can have is a tear gas gun, can of Mace, or one of the new disabling aerosol sprays. A tear gas gun costs between two and five dollars and is shaped like a fountain pen. Guns come in single or double-shot models and shoot shells the same size as a thirty-eight caliber revolver. They will stop man or beast at ten feet. Pointblank they will drop a man to his knees and disable him long enough for you to escape. They also give off the same loud report as a large bore pistol, which will not only scare the attacker but attract attention as well.

The pen-like tear gas gun can be carried unnoticed in the hand with the hammer in cocked position without any danger of it firing accidentally.

Mace is a disabling spray which is widely accepted and used by all police agencies. It comes in a slim spray can about five inches high.

The new aerosol sprays squirt a stream of fluid which literally smells like a skunk, stains skin and clothing with a bright red, orange, or green dye not easily removed without repeated washings, and which burns and irritates the skin and eyes. The only drawback is that the stream must be squirted directly into the face to disable an attacker.

These weapons should be carried *in the hand* when in an unprotected area or whenever you feel you may be in danger. Don't wait until you are attacked, or see you are going to be, to get it out of your purse. The rapist is not going to allow you this leeway.

If you are attacked or are certain you are going to be, shoot as quickly as you can. If you are using the tear gas gun, aim for the upper chest. The gas will spread to the face as soon as it is fired, and the chest is a larger target than the face.

The Mace need only be sprayed in the general direction to be effective.

As soon as any of these are used, flee in the opposite direction as quickly as possible. If not, the gas will have the same disabling effect on you as on the attacker.

Office buildings and elevators are a growing target

for rapists. When entering an elevator, exercise caution toward lone male occupants. When pushing your floor button, push three or four others as well. Then if you are attacked, the elevator will automatically stop at the other floors where help may wait. Also, if attacked, try to push as many buttons as possible, including any alarm button.

Women, if you are attacked, regardless of the location or circumstances, you should first try to discourage the man from raping you. Claiming pregnancy, menstruation, or venereal disease might cut him off at the pass.

The best action you can take, especially if a man is trying to force you into an automobile, is simply to fake fainting and collapse on the spot. It is the one reaction the rapist is totally unprepared for. It might very well curb his appetite for sex since he gets no reaction from his victim.

If the attacker has a dangerous weapon, you should not cry out or fight as long as the man is able to harm you. But if there is no weapon, and you must first be very certain, you should fight back with everything available and scream as loudly as you can. Remember, though, your reaction and/or resistance will depend on individual circumstances.

Hat pins, umbrellas, and pocketbooks are good defensive weapons. And do not forget fingernails and teeth, which are always present when no other weapon is available.

Eyes, neck, the area just below the rib cage, and the groin are the most effective places to strike. As soon as you are free of the attacker, you should run for help. *Never fight when you can run.*

After the Fact

Always call the police, immediately after an assault or rape, regardless of the circumstances. I cannot overemphasize *always*. Many rapists are free today because the victims were either too embarrassed or too scared to report the attack. They did not want their family and friends to know. This reticence is understandable. But there is no need for uninvolved individuals to know. Most newspapers throughout the country have been prevented, by either the state law or the professional courtesy of publishers, from printing the names of rape victims in the press at the time of the attack or when the case goes to trial.

Victims waiting for police to arrive should not change clothes, take a bath, apply fresh make-up, rearrange hair, or douche. The latter is the most important, since most rape cases must be medically sustained.

Assuming the rapist is captured, identified, indicted, and scheduled for trial, the victim should attend the trial. It is virtually impossible to convict a rapist without the testimony of the victim. In fact, merely appearing in court may be all that is needed. Ninety percent of all criminal cases which come to court are settled without a jury trial. When the culprit is confronted with the evidence and sees the witnesses are in court, he usually pleads guilty in exchange for a sentence the district attorney and his attorney agree upon, and the judge accepts. However, the woman must appear in court, lest the case be thrown out and the rapist freed to strike again.

The laws governing rape prosecution are grossly unfair to the victim. But with the proper persistence on the part of individual citizens and women's rights organizations, the laws can and will be changed.

8. Vice Crime

Gambling, prostitution, narcotics, and in an earlier era, bootlegging, are often referred to as *victimless crimes*. Such crimes involve illegal activities in which the victim either sides with the criminal in defiance of the law, or is in fact the criminal himself. This category of crime, therefore, supposedly boasts no victim.

However, is there not always a victim? The naive runaway schoolgirl who is taken in by a satanic procurer and forced to sell her body; the daily numbers player who drains his family income to support the local crime syndicate; the drug addict who ruins his mind, body, and spirit in an upward spiraling hunt for ever greater excitement—are not all of these victims of a sort? They are indeed the architects of their own disaster. Nevertheless, they cannot be ignored.

Whenever newspapers report crackdowns on vices such as gambling and prostitution, a certain percentage of the public will cry out for the police to stop arresting the gamblers, pimps, and prostitutes and to direct attention to more serious street crimes. Anyone making such an adverse statement is either himself involved in illegal vice, or not very well informed. For if crime breeds crime, and indeed it does, then gambling and prostitution are a hatchery.

Gambling

The "rags to riches" theme seems to be the elusive dream of every gambler. Numbers lotteries, sporting parleys, dog and horse racing, and the gleaming casinos of Las Vegas–all promise the proverbial rainbow and the subsequent pot of gold for the lucky winner. But more often than not, "riches to rags" is the name of the gambling game.

Most individuals begin gambling, or betting, as it is then called, before they start to school. At first the bets are small–candy, cokes, who takes out the garbage, and so on. By the time they reach their teens they are "matching" for their lunch money in the school rest rooms, tossing change to the wall, or shooting dice on the corner while waiting for the school bus.

Many high school graduates, especially males, enlist in the armed services and find poker games in the lonely barracks a momentary escape from reality. Each payday they exchange their paychecks for outstanding IOUs. When they are discharged three or four years later they are still broke.

At this stage in life another awareness seems to dawn on most people. New goals and objectives are sought, families begun. And with this awareness, for many, all gambling desires fade and eventually vanish.

For others, their gambling desire escalates into obsession. For some of these the compulsion for gambling will increase until they are losing more than their legal income, always hoping for that one big win which will allow them to break even or soar to riches. It seems inevitable, however, that the compulsive gambler turns to illegal activity to meet his mounting debts. Or, he turns to the loan shark, which in many cases can bring an equally unpleasant fate.

Interest rates and late charges are high at the loan

shark. Fifty to 100 percent interest, compounded weekly, is not unusual. If the debtor fails to make an interest payment, he may be subject to beatings and broken bones. If he finds he can no longer work because of sustained injuries, his wife or daughter may be forced into prostitution to pay his debts. *Is this not a crime?*

If the gambler has more courage than brains, he may find himself criminally involved: embezzling company funds; burglarizing homes and turning the merchandise over to the loan shark; with a gun in his hand sticking up liquor stores and gas stations, facing a twenty-year prison sentence; or face down in the street with the gun in his hand and a bullet in his head. *Is this not a crime?*

Many gamblers never reach this plateau of obsession or desperation. These are the average working men and women who bet on daily numbers lotteries, sporting parleys, and raffles when given the opportunity. Perhaps the sum is as small as fifty cents per workday on the numbers game, and a dollar a week for a raffle ticket on a new color television, which is probably stolen. It all seems so inconsequential. However, if the total investment for an entire year were computed, the sum would feed a family of four for a month. *Is this not a crime?*

Prostitution

Most people think of the world's oldest profession in the sense of $100-per-hour, Madison Avenue types of call girls living in the splendor of Hollywood-style apartments. And of pimps in their leather maxi-coats, widebrim hats cocked deuce-tray upon their heads, five-carat diamond clusters sparkling at every movement of their pinkie fingers, slightly extended from the padded steering wheels of their $25,000 El Dorados. These lifestyles do exist, in fact, as anyone who has ever been in the vicinity of 42nd Street and Broadway in New York City can testify. However, for each pimp and prostitute who reaches this supreme status, if it can be called that, 10,000 fall by the wayside.

Most prostitutes end up in county workhouses or penitentiaries, at drug addiction clinics and homes for unwed mothers, on abortion tables and in cemeteries, instead of in the penthouses they imagined.

A pimp is more likely to be tyrannical and despotic than tender and discreet. He reduces his women to the position of pawns in other people's games, where, like most pawns, they find themselves sacrificed to larger interests. He strips them of pride, dignity, and individualism. When he tires of a woman he sells her to another pimp like a head of livestock at the market. Or when her natural beauty has faded and her features can no longer be renovated by cosmetics, he casts her aside like an old shoe.

There are, of course, women who have chosen to be prostitutes because of economics, but they are few. There are others who have children, are deserted and destitute, and chose prostitution *only* over starvation. These cases number in the thousands. It is a pitiful society that does not offer an alternative to the woman having to choose between the two. But the mass of women who enter into prostitution do so through trickery on the part of the pimp.

Pimps are always on the lookout for runaway girls at bus depots or for the girl just graduated from high school who arrives in the big city for the first time. Such men know these girls are usually broke and hungry, for affection as well as nourishment. The pimp poses as a Good Samaritan and offers the young lady a place to stay for a few days. If she accepts, half the battle is won.

For the next several days the girl feels like a queen. The pimp treats her as gently as he would a flower, never really touching for fear of bruising. He buys her clothes, has her hair styled at a beauty parlor, lets her drive his

Cadillac, and takes her to all the places she always wanted to go.

After a few days he makes love to her in a tender way she has never before known. He tells her he loves her, and she believes him. She thinks she loves him also. Two wonderful weeks pass, weeks of living and loving as she had never known or thought possible.

Then one day her lover comes home early. Every morning he had been leaving for "work" and returning in the evening. She knows something must be wrong. Her lover tells her he has been fired from his job and is worried because he has bills due. She offers to help any way she can, but he refuses and promises to think of something.

Several days pass and her lover still says he cannot find a job. He asks, and she agrees, to visit his "ex-boss" and ask him to give her lover another chance.

The lover takes her to his ex-boss's apartment and leaves. The ex-boss, as it turns out, is as handsome and charming as her lover, and she finds herself at ease and having a drink, just before she passes out.

She awakens a short time later to find herself nude and in bed with her lover's ex-boss making love to her. She tries to struggle and doesn't understand how she got there. Sometime during the struggle she learns the man making love to her is a skillful lover, and she stops fighting.

Afterwards, the man tucks a $100 bill into her purse and leaves her alone with her reaction. She locks herself in the bathroom and tries to wash away the evidence. Perhaps she cries awhile. When she is ready to leave she checks herself in the mirror and is surprised to find her first act of prostitution has produced no visible change.

Returning to the apartment where her lover is waiting, she rushes into his arms and tells him the whole story. He says he is sorry, but asks for the money, adding that they need it.

A few days later, he asks her to go see his ex-boss again. She doesn't want to, but goes anyway. This time there are no preliminaries or formalities. He makes love to her again and gives her the now customary $100 bill.

Soon her lover has become her pimp, and she is introduced to more and more men. But now her customers are not so handsome, skillful, or gentle. Some are not even of her own race.

By the end of the first month she has graduated from one customer per week to ten per night. She never sees the money the men pay her pimp, who is now all business. If she does not feel like "working" he whips her with a coat hanger. She learns her pimp's "ex-boss" was actually only another pimp.

She becomes depressed so her pimp gives her amphetamines to make her feel better. When she can't sleep he gives her barbiturates. Soon she is taking pills to stay awake at night and more pills to sleep during the daytime. When her body builds up a resistance to the pills, she starts injecting drugs directly into her veins. Later, she starts using heroin.

By now she is completely trapped. Her pimp is her god. He controls her every move as if she was a puppet. She cannot leave him because he supplies her dope, fifty dollars worth a day. She is too scared to report him to the police. When she discovers she has gonorrhea she does not tell her pimp for fear of another beating. She continues to sell her body.

Six months after coming to live with the pimp she realizes she is a pregnant, venereal disease-carrying heroin addict. Still she does not tell her pimp. When she begins to show obvious signs of pregnancy, the pimp takes her to a doctor. When he learns her overall condition, he beats her and throws her into the street with only the clothes on her back. It is cheaper and easier to break in a new girl than to renovate the old one.

From here the girl has two ways she can go–to a hospital for treatment, or suicide. Far too many take the quick and easy way out–suicide.

Is this not a crime?

Narcotics

Booze and women will sell when the children are going hungry. This is an old and true saying in the criminal world. However, in today's version, I am sure the word *narcotics* would be substituted for *booze.* The booze era, sometimes recalled with nostalgia as a time of speakeasies and flappers, bathtub gin and armor-plated cars, came to an end with the repeal of the Eighteenth Amendment in 1933.

The criminals, especially those involved in organized crime, were forced into new fields. In the late thirties and early forties one group after another struggled to gain control of the expanding, lucrative territories of labor racketeering and gambling.

Labor racketeering and gambling activities, however, could not reap the monumental profits that Prohibition had delivered. During the twenties Al Capone netted a reputed $150 million in one year, a record yearly income for a single individual to this day.

So the criminal element set out in search of an alternate source to supplement a deflated income. The search took criminals across the Atlantic Ocean and the Mediterranean Sea, into the mountains which ring the central plateau of Turkey. There, they found another kind of intoxicant, a derivative of opium, made from the bitter, dried juice of unripe capsules called opium poppies–*heroin.* In the decades since it has acquired many aliases: smack, H, scag, horse, and many others. Some call it damnation; the addicts call it God. It remains the king of all illegitimate drugs.

Through the years, the trafficking of heroin and other narcotics has become a highly dangerous, and therefore, immensely profitable business. From ports of entry—such as Los Angeles, California; Brownsville, Texas; Savannah, Georgia; Fort Lauderdale, Florida; and New York City—to the addict on the street, the cost increases as much as 2000 percent.

Since the drug must be as small as possible for transportation purposes, most heroin enters the country 100 percent pure. It cannot, of course, be sold directly to the addict on the street at such potency. The amount of pure heroin it would take to cover the head of a pin would be enough to overdose and kill a heavy user. So each time the drug changes hands, it is *cut* to reduce potency and at the same time increase volume and profit.

The importer will sell a pound of 100 percent heroin for $25,000. After paying all expenses of manufacturing, smuggling, and 10 percent commission to the front man for selling the drug, therefore protecting himself against detection, a profit of $20,000 remains for the importer.

The man who bought the drug will mix nine pounds of reducer, usually milk-sugar, to the one pound of heroin. This brings the heroin content level down to 10 percent and increases the volume to ten pounds.

He now sells the addictive drug to junkies, (who sell drugs to the addicts to support their own drug habits) either by the ounce or teaspoon. One ounce sells for $800, a total of $128,000 for the original, inflated pound. If the heroin is sold by the spoon, which takes much longer and is extremely risky since this means dealing with more lower-class people, at $200 per, the total return is $224,000. The high profits are the reward for dealing with the unreliable and treacherous junkie.

The junkie will again cut the heroin by at least one

part to give it a final 5 percent content (the average is between 3 and 6 percent pure), giving him twice the amount he purchased. Some of this he will divide into five- and ten-dollar bags which he will sell to the addicts on the street to retain operating capital and pay his few expenses. The rest he will use to maintain his own addiction. For the junkie, there is no progressing profit.

Unless financially independent, he inevitably turns to some form of criminal activity to support a $50- to $300-a-day drug habit. Sixty-five percent of those who fill our prisons today are there because of drug-related offenses.

The reason for the high cost of addiction is the quick establishment of biological tolerance for the opiate drug. The result, of course, is it takes larger and larger quantities to produce the same effects: analgesia (relief of pain); sedation (freedom from anxiety, muscular relaxation and decreased activity); and euphoria (a sense of well-being and contentment).

But when the drug is withdrawn, the body and mind do not merely cease to enjoy the above-mentioned momentary relief from reality. The physical reactions to withdrawal are varied and violent. Yawning, sneezing, crying, running nose, goose flesh, rapid pulse, sexual orgasms, increased blood pressure, dilated pupils, hot and cold flashes, nausea, vomiting, diarrhea, muscular spasms—all strike addicts with a painfulness which often takes them to the brink of self-destruction for a period of ten days to two weeks. The desire to avoid withdrawal symptoms and pains becomes a crutch for continuing use of the drug.

Very few addicts begin with heroin or other opiate-derived drugs which can be eaten or smoked as well as injected. Many begin with the controversial marijuana, which has been studied, attacked, and condemned *ad infinitum.* There are those who are content to remain on this first rung of the proverbial ladder of drugs. However, many feel they must seek the ultimate high and graduate to hashish, amphetamines, barbiturates, MDA, THC, LSD, and cocaine, frequently building them into lifestyles which explicitly and deliberately reject the traditional values of the dominant society.

Of all so-called victimless crimes, in which neither the sanctity of the body nor private property is attacked, the illegal use of narcotics is perhaps the most illuminating as the concept of crime as a form of perversity emerges with special clarity.

Gambling, prostitution, and narcotics form the foundation of organized crime. The capital derivatives from these sources amount to an estimated $30 billion a year—a toll greater than the combined net profits of the 100 largest corporations in America, including General Motors, General Electric, and U.S. Steel—unquestionably overshadowing the losses due to larceny, robbery, and burglary.

Therefore, so-called victimless crimes are no less than generators which produce the power to create crime.

Epilogue

In the foregoing chapters we have explored many crimes, their causes, and their preventions. If the prevention methods are applied as described, they will undoubtedly reduce the odds of victimization. However, there is one other area of crime prevention which is of equal importance: restoring and/or building the convicted criminal offender into a useful person before returning him to society, and lending him a guiding hand after he is rejoined.

It is presumptuous to assume that merely locking up a convicted person for a given number of years until the revenge motif of "an eye for an eye" is satisfied, then releasing him with the command "go and sin no more" will deter crime and/or cure and rehabilitate the offender. Punishment will not always prevent crime—just as medicine will not always prevent death. The judicial and penal systems, therefore, resemble those of the medical profession. The consequence of usage lies in the technique applied rather than the execution of the act.

When a convicted person is sent to prison, it should be *as* punishment for the crime, not *for* punishment. The objective of confinement should be not only to protect society against the criminal but, equally, to ready the offender for a useful and productive life upon release.

The phrase *prison reform* is widely used but not very well defined. Prison reform has represented everything from instilling good work habits in offenders, to renovating an outdated penitentiary, to reorganizing prison administrations. However, prison reform seems to be a reality more in lip service than in practice.

To emphasize how little our correctional systems have changed and how far they must develop before being able to effectively transform the criminal offender into a useful citizen, we should view the "Declaration of Principles" for the treatment of prisoners, as set forth by the American Prison Congress in Cincinnati, Ohio:

(1) Reformation, not vindictive suffering, should be the purpose of penal treatment of prisoners.
(2) Rewards should be provided for good conduct.
(3) The chief obstacles to prison reform are the political appointment of prison officials, and the instability of management.
(4) The prisoners should be made to realize that their destiny is in their own hands.
(5) Prison officials should be trained for their jobs.
(6) Religion and education are cited as the most important agencies of reform.
(7) Prison discipline should be such as to gain the will of the prisoner and conserve his self-respect.
(8) The aim of the prisons should be to make industrious free people rather than orderly and obedient Prisoners.
(9) Industrial training should be provided for.
(10) Prisons should be small and there

should be separate institutions for different types of offenders.

(11) There should be idemnification of prisoners who are later discovered to be innocent.

(12) There should be revision of the laws relating to treatment of insane criminals.

(13) A more adequate prison architecture should be developed providing sufficiently for air and sunlight, as well as for prison hospitals, schools, etc.

(14) The social training of prisoners should be facilitated through proper associations, and the abolition of the silence rules.

(15) Society at large should be made to realize its responsibility for crime conditions.

The request for these reforms is heard often. Usually the demand echoes in the aftermath of prison revolt, after the screams of hostages and the roar of destructive fires have died away. The sadness of the fact is that when the American Prison Congress met in Cincinnati to establish these very guidelines, it was in 1870–110 years ago. Over a century has passed, over a trillion dollars have been lost in crime, and we still have the same problems today as we had then.

Prisons are authoritarian communities and by their very nature must remain so. They should not be, however, merely warehouses for retaining criminals, or worse, schools of crime where the inmate learns the trades of his fellow comrades. When pickpockets, shoplifters, drunks, car thieves, burglars, robbers, murderers, and sex offenders are lumped together by the thousands, to work, eat, and sleep in intimate coexistence for years on end, the emerging individual is often a combination of two or more of his associates.

As noted earlier, people with destructive impulses, such as murderers, do not always commit crimes against property, and vice versa. Therefore they should be placed in separate institutions according to their crimes. When they are mixed, the association produces criminals capable of violent acts as well as crimes against property.

There are over 250,000 men and 20,000 women in federal and state prisons throughout the United States. With the exception of the federal prison system, it costs more to keep each person in prison than to enroll him in a major university. But the federal prison system is different simply because it features self-supporting industries within the institutions.

Each institution manufactures a product in great demand by the federal government, and at the same time teaches the inmates a useful trade. By doing so, it saves the taxpayers the astronomical cost of maintaining the prison.

The profits from the industries are returned to the institutions for maintaining the facility, expanding vocations, and paying the working inmates a small salary (ranging from twenty-one to sixty-five cents per hour). Three-fourths of inmates' salaries is placed in savings accounts or, if they prefer, in government bonds, to be given to them at the time of their release. In a few years this can amount to several thousand dollars, somewhat better than the traditional gray suit, bus ticket and twenty-five dollars with which to build a new life.

Several states, and specifically Colorado, have adopted new correctional programs, with the latter recognized as the best in the nation. When an inmate enters one of their institutions, he is diagnosed, analyzed, and classified in accordance with the nature of his offense, past record, education, vocational training, and ambitions. The result is a behavior contract drawn up between the institution and the inmate, agreed to and signed by both. The contract lists the accomplishments deemed necessary to build the inmate into a useful person. If the inmate has little or no education or vocation, he must complete a high school equivalency course and get his diploma, or graduate from a vocational training course of his choice. Those with drug problems must attend drug therapy classes. Alcoholics must join Alcoholics Anonymous. Emotionally troubled inmates are enrolled in psycho- or group therapy.

The maximum completion time of the programs ranges from one to five years or more. If the inmate wants to complete his program in less than the maximum time, he may do so. But any violation of institutional rules will result in additional time being added to the program.

The last six months of every program is conducted on work-release; the inmate works at a regular job in society during working hours and returns to the institution during off-hours. Part of his salary is paid to the institution for his upkeep and transportation to and from his job. The remainder is placed in a savings account until he is released.

When the inmate is released, he not only has a modest savings account but also has established goals and work habits.

If an inmate refuses to accept and sign a behavior contract, and negotiations fail to resolve differences, he can simply serve out his maximum sentence without the benefit of sentence reduction for good time. There is, of course, the possibility of an inmate agreeing to the contract merely to reduce the time he is to spend in prison, and indeed this happens.

Even if effective rehabilitation programs are available, there will always be some offenders who choose not to be converted. The old saying, "You can lead a horse to water but you can't make him drink," seems to be composed precisely for this situation.

On the other hand, there is always the possibility the inmate will improve his attitude during the rehabilitation program, even if that had not been his first objective.

The Colorado behavior contract is undoubtedly better than the so-called rehabilitation of the road gangs of the South, the cotton fields of the Midwest, the bleak fortress of San Quentin where inmates are constantly confined to cells, and in the license tag plants of many other states. It is unrealistic to make prisoners dig ditches, work on farms, and stamp out auto tags for years on end, and to expect them then to return to a normal and productive life.

But the problem of rehabilitating criminals does not end at the prison gates. Only the first step stops there. The very community to which he will return must understand and support postprison rehabilitation. Those who shun the ex-convict with a pessimistic attitude, and the companies who flatly refuse to give ex-convicts a chance to prove themselves—all are tightening the lid on the progress of rehabilitation. By doing so, they may be causing an optimistic ex-convict to change his attitude and seek relief in alcohol or drugs, committing another crime out of desperation in the end. Therefore it is just as important for the community to change its attitude toward the ex-convict, as it is for the inmate to reassess his valuation of the lives and property of others while in prison.

For centuries we have made the punishment fit the crime, a moral imbalance that must be redressed. We have precedents that have produced equations between harm done and harm returned. With the convenient, if not necessarily logical, measurement of time, we have made so many years of imprisonment or probation worth this or that illegal act. A life taken has meant a life taken in return. When, however, we cease to cling to this retributive viewpoint as our major goal, and instead, become primarily interested in rehabilitating the offender and preventing crime, we will enter a new dimension and may begin to see our skyrocketing crime rate taper into a downward trend.

The cost of crime is a luxury society cannot afford. But if we are both persistent and wise, someday we can and will have the best of both worlds: security and convenience.